LIGHTHOUSES OF WALES

WARREN KOVACH

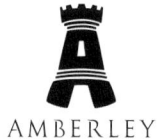

AMBERLEY

Cover images, front: South Stack lighthouse; *back*: Bardsey Island lighthouse.

First published 2025

Amberley Publishing
The Hill, Stroud,
Gloucestershire, GL5 4EP

www.amberley-books.com

ISBN: 978 1 3981 2062 4 (print)
ISBN: 978 1 3981 2063 1 (ebook)

British Library Cataloguing in Publication Data.
A catalogue record for this book is available from the British Library.

Typeset in 10pt on 13pt Celeste.
Origination by Amberley Publishing.
Printed in the UK.

Appointed GPSR EU Representative: Easy Access System Europe Oü, 16879218
Address: Mustamäe tee 50, 10621, Tallinn, Estonia
Contact Details: gpsr.requests@easproject.com, +358 40 500 3575

Contents

Introduction

The road leads from the port town of Holyhead and through the village of Llaingoch, skirting around the edge of the rocky prominence of Mynydd Twr (Holyhead Mountain). Past the hillside a right turn takes you further, towards the edge of the world. This is the path to the lighthouse at South Stack.

But it's not the edge of the world. There are ships and boats out there, mariners and fishermen trying to find their way to the next port, or to return home. They are always aware of the dangers, of the rocky coasts that could swallow up their ships. The lighthouse warns them of this danger and leads them on their way.

Today this road is well travelled by visitors taking in the dramatic views of the coast and lighthouse, as well as wildlife lovers heading to the nature reserve brimming with birds, insects and low-growing plants. In the past it was taken by the lighthouse keepers, returning to their post with provisions. At the end of the road, they would walk down the 400 steps carved into the rocky cliff face, across the swaying suspension bridge, into the tower and up the 100 steps to the lantern room of the lighthouse. As a tour guide, I am following in their footsteps, arriving for my shift taking curious visitors up those steps and talking about how wonderful lighthouses are.

I've been interested in the local history of my adopted home of Anglesey (Ynys Môn) for many years, and have written three books about it, which often focus on unusual and historic buildings. Lighthouses tick both these boxes, and I started tour guiding at South Stack lighthouse, on the rocky islet of Ynys Lawd, in 2021. Learning the history of this lighthouse gave me a greater appreciation of these structures, leading me to explore more of them in Wales. That has led to this book.

The coast of Wales is dotted with lighthouses. Some sit on rocks dangerously jutting out from the sea, some mark the ends of piers and breakwaters. Others rest on top of cliffs gazing out over the water. Lighthouses serve to guide ships through coastal waters. They lead ocean-going ships to the major ports such as Milford Haven, Swansea, Holyhead and Liverpool. They also warn mariners of dangerous coasts and looming rocky islets. This book takes you into the world of the lighthouse, explaining how they were built, how they work and who worked in them.

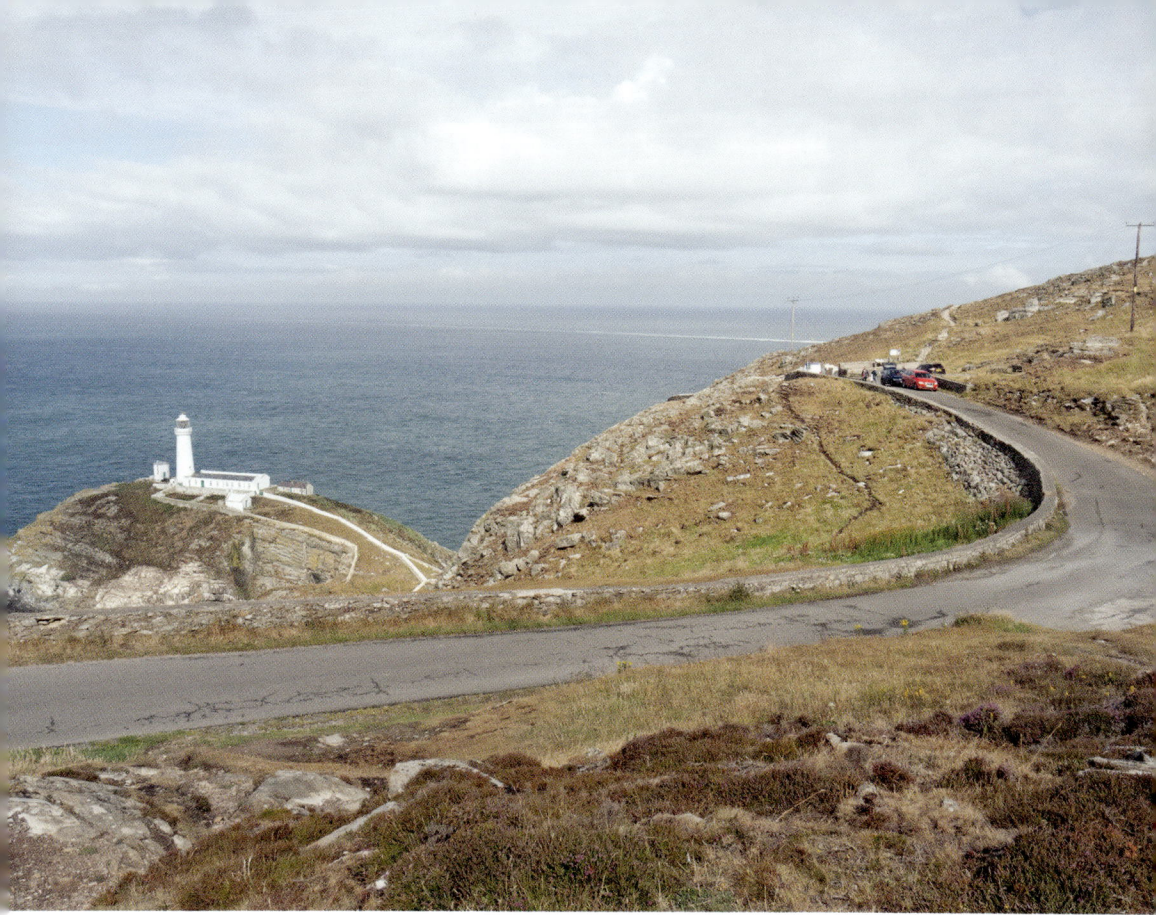

The road leading to South Stack lighthouse.

A lighthouse (*goleudy* in Welsh, from *golau*, 'light' and *tŷ*, 'house') can be defined as a building or structure containing a light that acts as a navigational aid and warning of hazards for mariners. For this book I will mainly be including those structures where you can go inside, like a house. There are many other lights that are on poles, solid masonry towers or metal scaffolding structures, which can be considered beacons. A few of the more interesting ones of these will make an appearance.

Rather than taking a gazetteer approach, discussing each lighthouse in turn, this book will talk about different aspects of lighthouses in general, using specifics from Welsh lighthouses to illustrate the points. An appendix at the end lists all the Welsh lighthouses, with details of locations, dates, etc.

This book is written with the general public in mind, the reader who may be interested in the historic buildings of Wales and wants to know more about these unusual structures that surround our coast. It places Welsh lighthouses in the exciting, bigger picture of innovative technology leading to improved maritime safety around the world. The Further Reading section at the end of this volume lists a number of books that delve more deeply into the development, construction and working of the lighthouses.

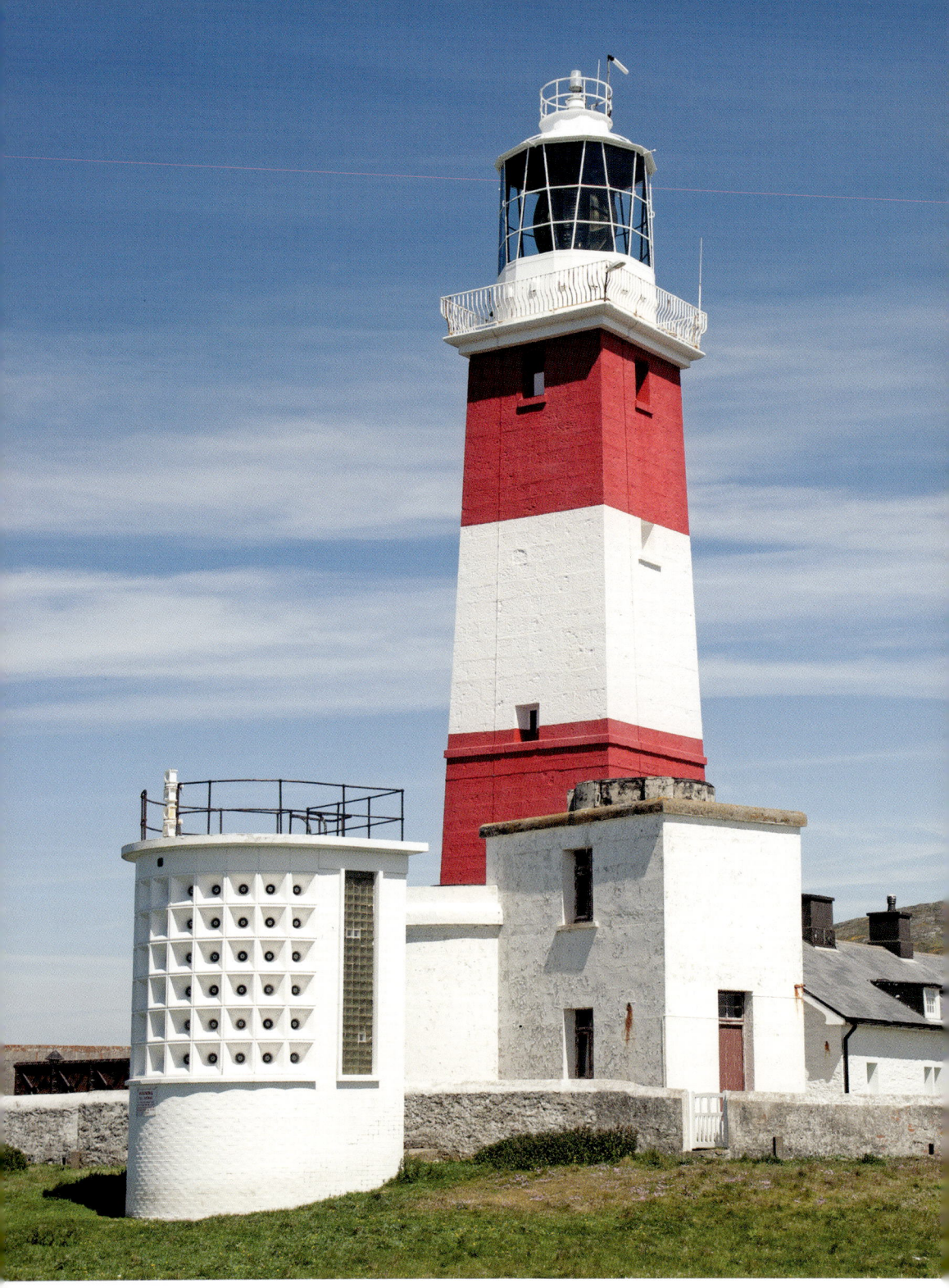

Bardsey lighthouse.

CHAPTER 1

Early Lights

Humans have taken to the water for millennia. Navigation at sea, both in the early days and to a lesser extent today, relies on observations of the position of the sun, moon and stars, as well as identifiable landmarks when close to the coast. It would be an obvious move for sea-going people to develop specific structures, with lights to enhance their visibility, particularly at night. However, before 2,300 years ago there is no documentary evidence of lighthouses.

Around 280 BC a magnificent structure was raised on the island of Pharos, at the entrance to the port of Alexandria, in modern-day Egypt. It was such a remarkable structure that it was widely described in the writings of Greek, Roman and Arab authors, and became known as one of the Seven Wonders of the World, alongside the Great Pyramid of Giza and the Hanging Gardens of Babylon. The Pharos of Alexandria is the first lighthouse to be historically documented and indeed gives its name to the study of lighthouses: pharology.

The construction of lighthouses soon spread around the Mediterranean, particularly with the expansion of the Roman Empire. In AD 43 they reached Britain, when Emperor Claudius built two lighthouses to mark the entrance to Dover Harbour. Remarkably, one of them still stands, nearly two millennia later, having been converted to a church tower in AD 1000.

There have been some suggestions about the existence of Roman lighthouses in Wales. Thomas Pennant, the eighteenth-century travel writer, naturalist and antiquarian, lived all his life in Whitford, Flintshire, near to an ancient circular tower on top of a hill, Mynydd y Garreg. In his history of the parish, he describes it as a Roman lighthouse, sited there to aid navigation into the River Dee towards the Roman fort of Deva (now Chester). However, later studies have shown that the stonework dates from the late sixteenth or early seventeenth centuries at the earliest, long after the Romans. It is likely that this tower, as well as three others along the coast, were erected as watch and signal towers to protect against pirate raids, which were common along this coast in the seventeenth century.

In Pennant's *A Tour in Wales* he describes visiting the Roman fort of Caer Gybi, in Holyhead, Anglesey. He notes that the remains of a circular tower on top of the nearby Mynydd Twr mountain has stonework and mortar like that at the fort, and concludes that

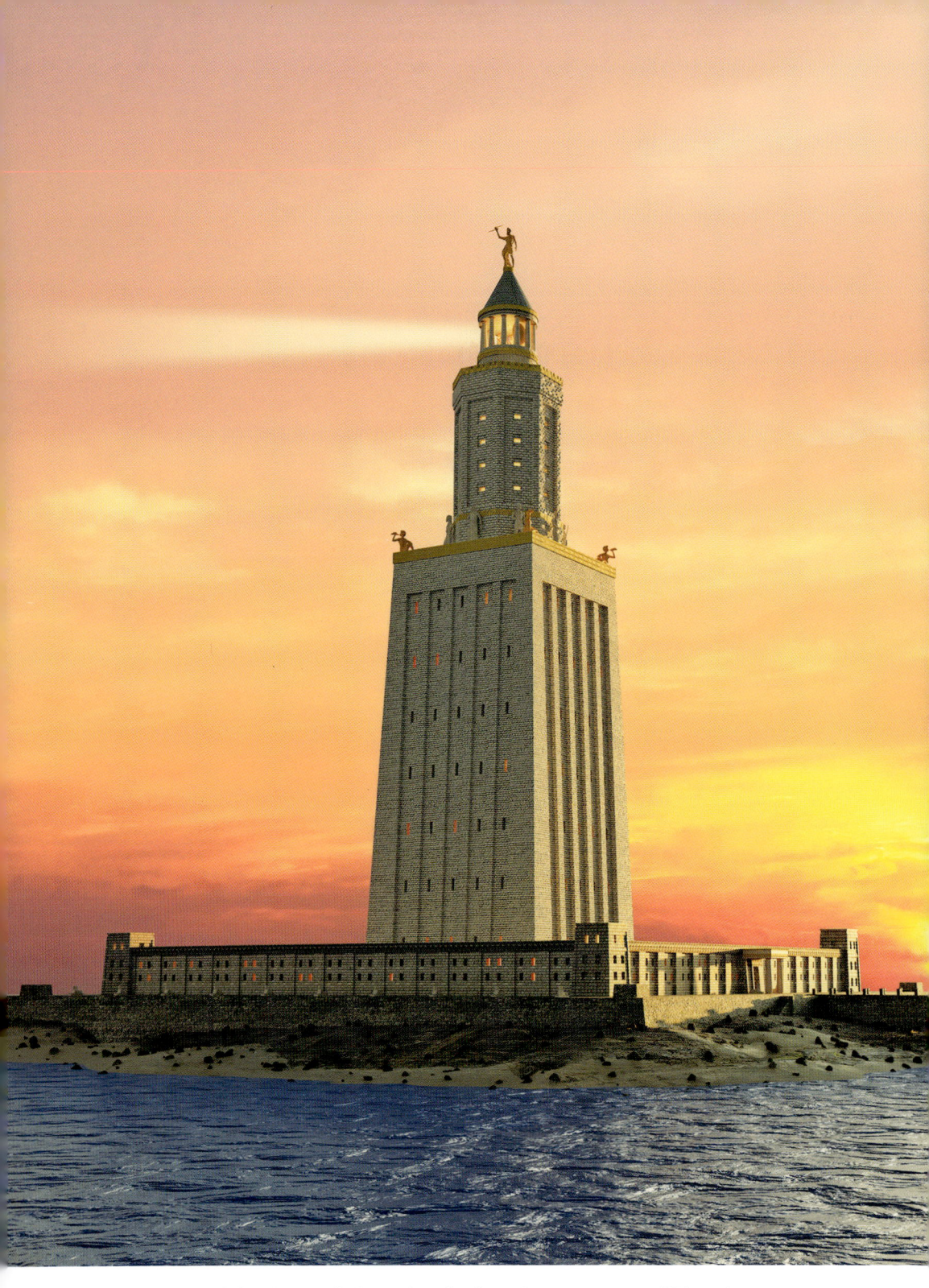

Reconstruction of the Pharos of Alexandria. (Wikimedia CC BY-SA 4.0/ Віщун)

it was also a Roman lighthouse, overlooking the Irish Sea. This has since been confirmed as a Roman structure but is more likely to have been a watch and signal tower.

The earliest definite record of a lighthouse in Wales is at St Ann's Head (Penrhyn Santes Ann in Welsh), on the approaches to Milford Haven, Pembrokeshire. This overlooks Mill Bay, which was the landing site in 1485 for Henry Tudor and his army, starting their march to Bosworth Field. After winning the battle and becoming King Henry VII, he ordered a chapel to be erected here to commemorate the landing. The round tower of this chapel was described in the next century as being a landmark for mariners. In 1662 Trinity House (the lighthouse authority in England and Wales; more about them later) gave permission for a light to be exhibited here. It may be that the existing chapel tower was used for this.

In 1713 local landowner Joseph Allen was granted permission to erect a new lighthouse tower here. He was also allowed to charge duty on passing ships to cover the costs of running the lighthouse. This was and still is the method of funding lighthouses; the duties would be collected at the next port and are based on the size of the ship. At the time the charge was one penny per ton for British ships and two pennies for foreign ones. Today Trinity House charge 45 pence per ton.

The second tower at St Ann's Head was placed at a precise point in relation to the first tower to improve their navigational use. When a ship is approaching the mouth of Milford Haven from the east, there are exposed rocks 700 m off Linney Head, the Toe and Crow Rocks, that present a hazard. However, if the ship's navigator can see that the two towers at St Ann's Head are lined up, one behind the other, he will know they are far enough away from the coast to avoid those rocks. This system of leading lights, where two or more lighthouses or beacons are placed to indicate routes of safe passage, is widely used around the world. Having two lights here was also useful for ocean-going ships approaching the British coast. The other major lighthouse at the time was a single light on the Isles of Scilly and distinguishing between the two sites allowed mariners to ensure they were on the right course.

The two original towers were replaced in 1800 by two new lighthouses, with the lower, easternmost one near the cliff edge. In 1844 this one was rebuilt to move it back a bit from

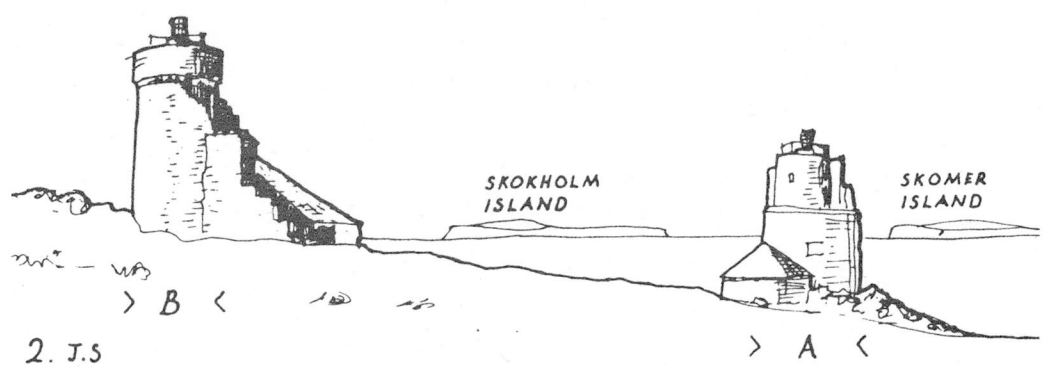

The original two towers at St Ann's Head, as depicted by John Smith, c. 1792. (Redrawn by Douglas B. Hague)

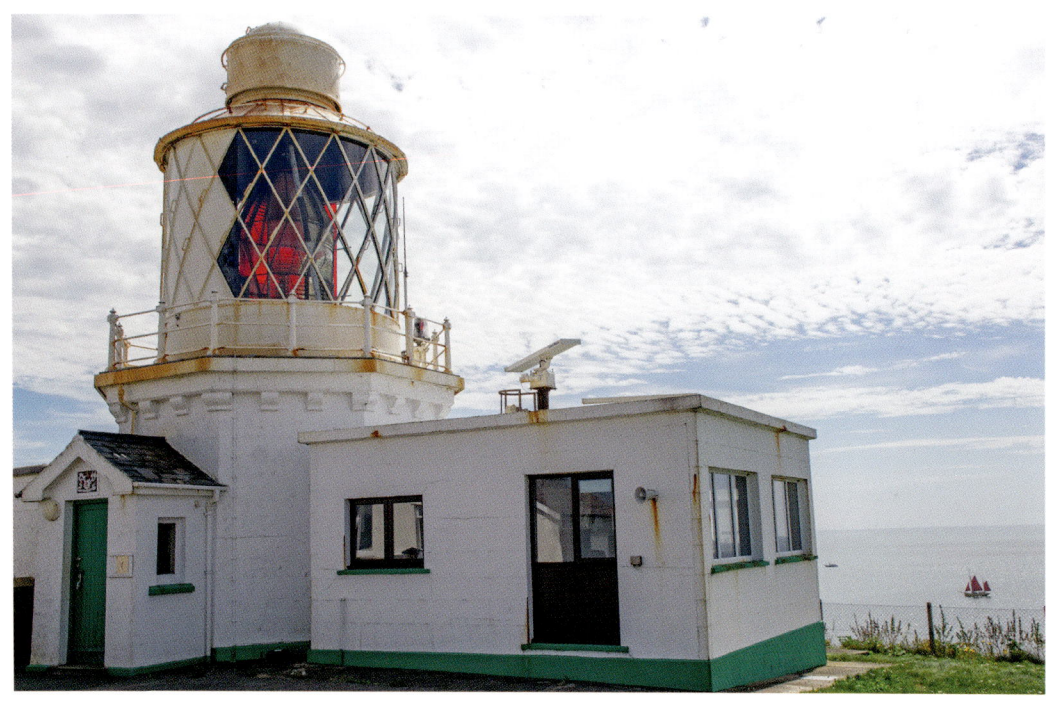

The active lower light at St Ann's Head.

the eroding cliff. This is now the active light, the other one having been decommissioned in 1910. The lantern was removed from the inactive tower during the Second World War and replaced with a lookout room.

Rising out of the Irish Sea, 3 km off the northwest extremity of Anglesey, are the rocky islets of the Skerries (Ynysoedd y Moelrhoniaid in Welsh, 'The Seal Islands'). These are right in the path of ships rounding the corner on their way across North Wales to Liverpool, and thus present a major hazard. As early as 1658 an attempt was made to build a lighthouse here. The business speculator Henry Hascard petitioned Cromwell's Council of State for permission to erect a private lighthouse, but the move was opposed by the official lighthouse authority, Trinity House. Another petition in 1709, by a group of shipowners led by Captain John Davison, was accepted by the government, establishing the principle that organisations other than Trinity House can erect lighthouses. However, this group never actually built it.

A few years later, in 1714, the islands were leased to William Trench, the youngest son of a wealthy landowner from Garbally, Co. Galway, Ireland. He was well connected to the Irish government and saw a business opportunity in building a lighthouse to aid shipping from Dublin to Liverpool. He was granted a patent from Queen Anne to erect the lighthouse and charge passing ships dues of one penny per ton in return for a £5 annual rent to the Crown.

Sadly, the lighthouse did not get off to a good start. Trench sent the first work party, which included his son Robert and six other men, out to the island with materials to begin construction. Tragedy struck as their boat was wrecked on the rocks, with the loss of all lives. This was a setback to his plans, but the lighthouse was eventually finished in November 1717. Standing 11 m high, the tower was topped with a brazier in which a coal fire was lit.

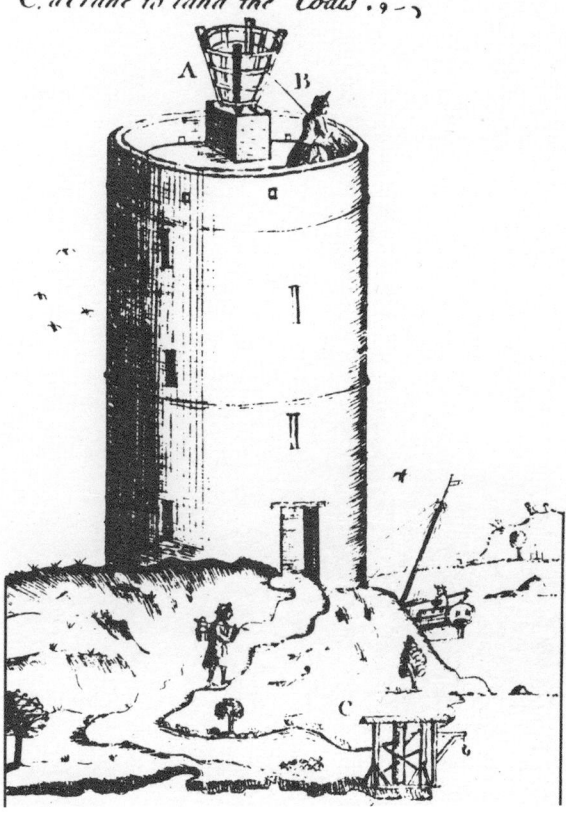

Drawing by Lewis Morris, 1748, probably depicting the Skerries lighthouse.

William Trench's business plans did not work out as well as he had hoped. He was seriously in debt when he died around 1726. The lighthouse was inherited by his daughter Anne and her husband the Revd Sutton Morgan. They were granted a new patent by Parliament allowing them to increase the dues paid by shipping, making it a much more viable commercial venture. It also gave them and their heirs this right in perpetuity. The lighthouse was inherited by his niece Rebecca Morgan, then by her nephew Morgen Jones, who rebuilt the tower in 1804. By the time it was inherited by his nephew, also called Morgen Jones, it was a very lucrative property indeed. In the early 1830s the lighthouse was making an annual profit of around £12,000 (£1.43 million in today's money).

In 1836 an Act of Parliament was passed that gave Trinity House the right to compulsorily purchase any lighthouses in England and Wales that were still in private hands. Trinity House's origins lie in medieval guilds of seamen and pilots, and in 1514 they were given a royal charter by Henry VIII. Their mission was, and still is, to improve navigational aids, to regulate and train pilots and sailors around the coast of England and Wales, and to look after the welfare of retired mariners. They built many of their own lighthouses, but also allowed private ones, like the Skerries, to be erected.

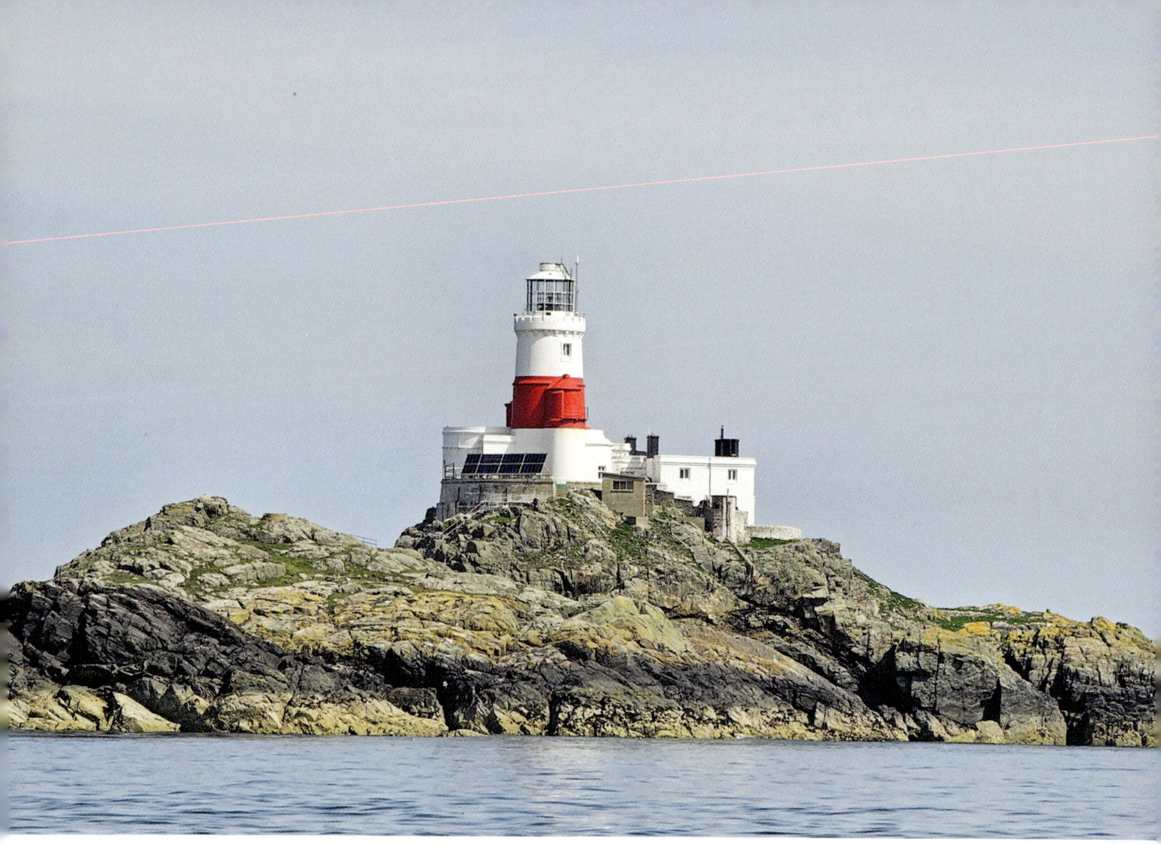

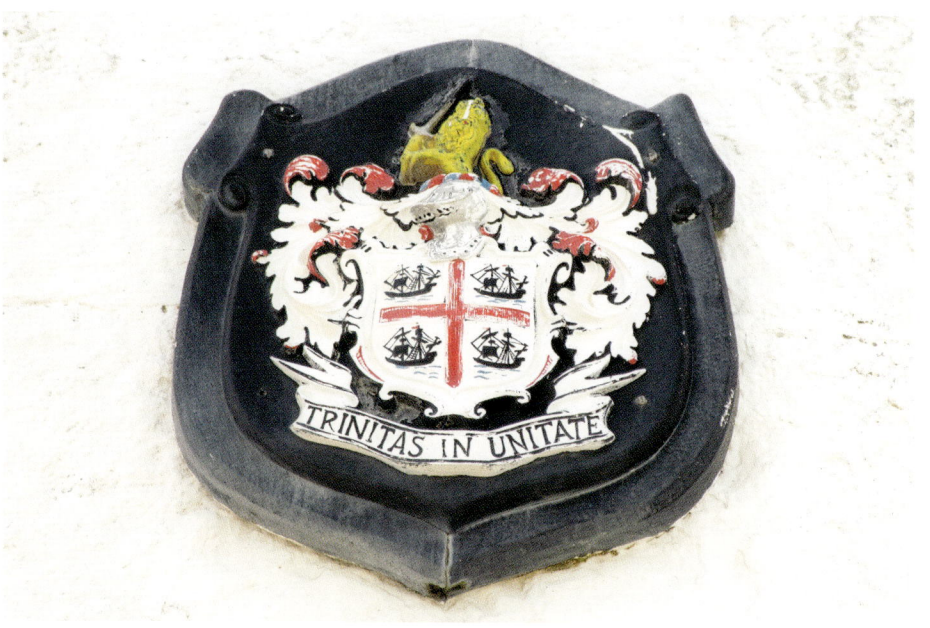

Skerries lighthouse.

Trinity House coat of arms at Nash Point lighthouse.

Unfortunately, the owners of many of these private lights focused more on profit rather than mariners' safety, and there was growing unease within the maritime community, particularly as sea-going trade increased across the British Empire. The 1836 Act allowed Trinity House to begin buying out the private lights to run them more effectively. However, some owners proved more resistant than others. Trinity House had to offer compensation to private owners to cover the expected profits for the remainder of their lease. The Morgan family had been granted the ownership of the Skerries lighthouse in perpetuity and they were demanding payment for what in effect was an infinite amount of future profit. After five years of negotiation Morgen Jones finally accepted compensation of the phenomenal amount of £444,984 (£52 million today).

It was twenty years after the lighting of the Skerries that the next lighthouse was built, at the opposite end of Wales. In the middle of the Bristol Channel, near Cardiff, sits a small and low-lying island, Flat Holm (Ynys Echni in Welsh). It has been occupied since the late Bronze Age and in the sixth century was the retreat of St Cadoc. A monastery was later founded there. This island and its nearby protruding rocks lie next to the main navigable channel leading into the Severn Estuary towards Bristol, presenting a challenge for mariners.

For many years the building of a lighthouse was discussed by ship owners and the Society of Merchant Venturers of Bristol. This led Society member John Elbridge to send a petition to Trinity House in 1733, asking for a light. This was rejected, but then in 1735 William Crispe of Bristol took out a ninety-nine-year lease on the island from the Earl

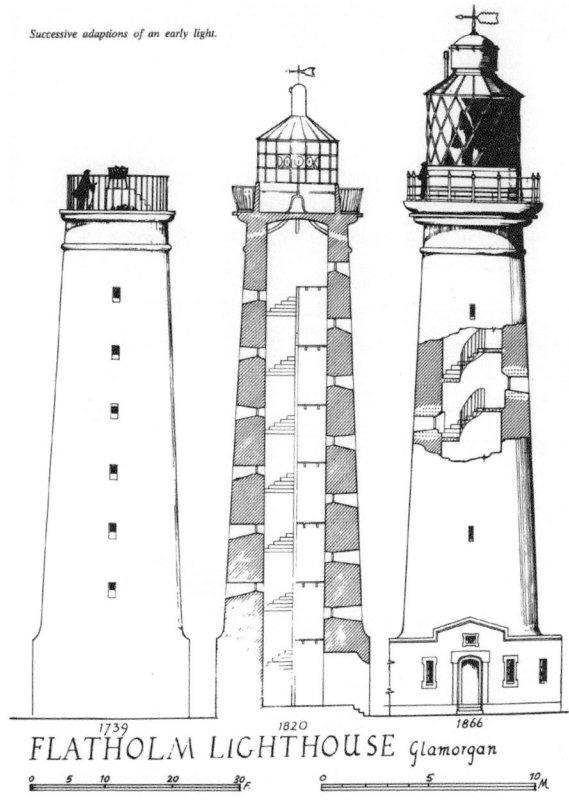

Successive adaptions of an early light.

FLATHOLM LIGHTHOUSE Glamorgan

The three stages of the Flat Holm lighthouse. (Douglas B. Hague)

of Bute. He again asked Trinity House to allow him to build a lighthouse, but his plans were also rejected. However, tragedy forced their hand as sixty soldiers were drowned when their vessel was wrecked nearby in 1736. The next year revised plans were presented to Trinity House and this time they were accepted. The tower was built and the coal brazier fire on top was lit on 25 March 1738.

As with the Skerries, the private owners of Flat Holm struggled to balance the cost of building and running the lighthouse with the income from duties. Crispe and his new partner Benjamin Lund went bankrupt around 1743 and the lease to the lighthouse was passed to Caleb Dickenson. It was run by him, his son and grandson (both called William) for many years, but local traders and mariners always complained about what they thought was an inadequate coal-fired light. In 1819 Trinity House signed an agreement with the younger William to improve the light and take over the maintenance of it. The top of the tower was rebuilt, with a new enclosed lantern room that housed an Argand lamp (an oil lamp, described in more detail later in Chapter 3). In 1823 Trinity House completely took over the lighthouse by buying out the remainder of the lease from the Dickensons for £15,838.10 (£1.75 million today). Various improvements were made to the lighthouse over the decades, including rebuilding the lantern again in 1866.

Towards the end of the eighteenth century a few more lighthouses sprouted on the Welsh coast. In 1776 work started on the Point of Ayr lighthouse (Y Parlwr Du in Welsh, 'The Black Parlour'), standing on the shore near Talacre, Flintshire, overlooking the entrance to the River Dee. The merchants of Chester were hoping to revive their port (which had declined over the years due to the silting up of the Dee and increased competition from nearby Liverpool) and included a lighthouse in their plans.

When first built the tower had two windows showing the light to the west along the North Wales coast and to the north approaching the estuary. In 1819 it was taken over by Trinity House, who rebuilt the lantern with glazing all around to provide a brighter light. This still didn't give a sufficiently visible beacon, so in 1844 they replaced it with a new piled structure built further out to sea on cast-iron cylinders driven into the sea floor, topped with living quarters and a lantern room. That structure was then replaced by a lightship in 1883. The tower, although no longer fulfilling its original purpose, still stands proudly on the beach. It is privately owned and has occasionally been used as a holiday home since the 1930s.

A more remarkable achievement in 1776 was the building of a lighthouse on the Smalls. This low-lying reef 29 km off the Pembrokeshire coast can easily be missed by a ship's lookout, leading to a sinking. In the 1760s John Phillips, the Master of St George's Dock in Liverpool, began contemplating a lighthouse on the Smalls. Many of the ships going past the Smalls were on their way to Liverpool, and wrecks there were felt strongly in the city. He was already interested in lighthouses as he was the agent for the proprietors of the Skerries.

Phillips eventually obtained a lease to the Smalls in 1774 and put out a call for design proposals. He wanted 'to build a lighthouse on the principal rock of the Smalls, of so singular a construction as to be known from all others in the world, as well by night as by day; to be known the moment it is seen and not to be mistaken for any other'. His chosen design was produced by Henry Whiteside, a young man whose usual profession was, oddly enough, musical instrument maker. Whiteside's vision was of an octagonal timber

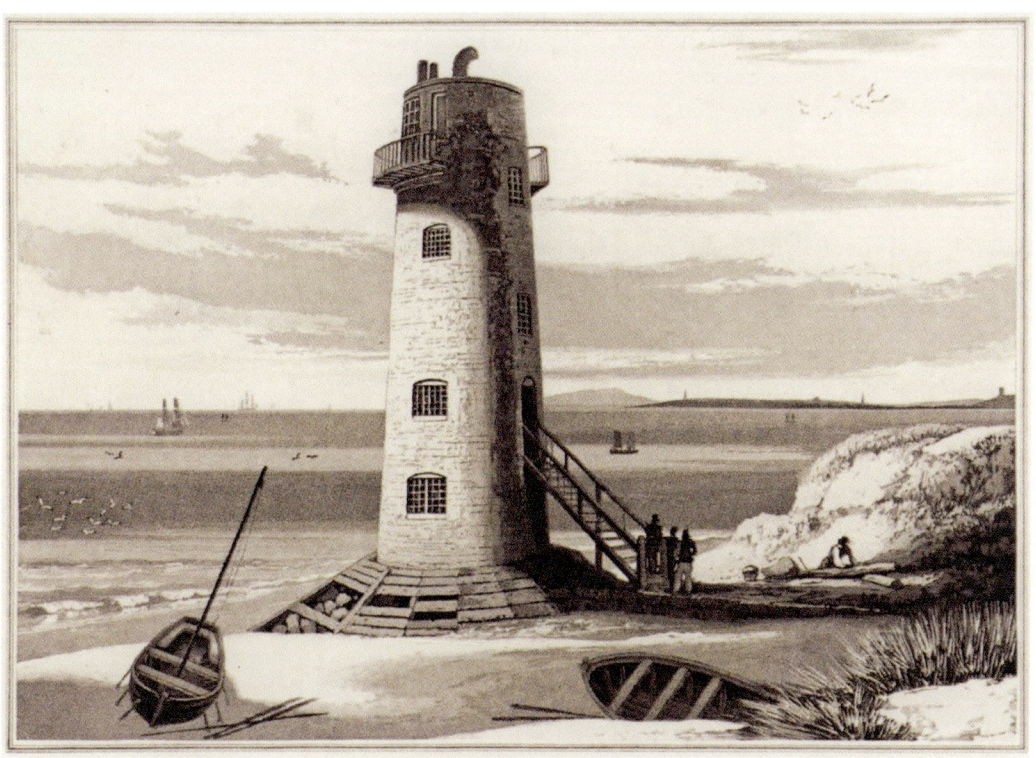

Point of Ayr lighthouse in 1815. (William Daniell)

structure, with living quarters topped by the lantern, all perched on timber posts, sunk into holes painstakingly drilled into the hard rock. Unlike a solid masonry tower, a piled design allows the force of the sea to pass through rather than hammering the entire structure.

On 17 June 1775 Whiteside and a group of labourers, including eight Cornish miners, set sail from Liverpool to the Smalls to begin the arduous task of drilling the holes for the posts. As the rocks were low lying and the waves regularly fierce, the amount of time they could spend there working was very limited. Often, they had to lash themselves to iron rings attached to the rock to avoid being swept away. Once they were finished the materials for the building and lantern were brought to nearby Solva Harbour, where they were built in a field. On completion, it was dismantled and transported out to the reef to be re-erected on top of the piles. The light was first lit in the summer of 1776.

Although the structure may seem flimsy, it survived its first winter, a very stormy one, albeit with some damage. Modifications were made, adding more supporting timbers and other repairs, and the structure continued in use until 1861. By this time, it had been taken over by Trinity House. Their consultant engineer James Walker erected a sleek new granite tower on the Smalls, gradually tapering upward to the lantern. Whiteside's tower was then demolished. Today's lighthouse is mostly unchanged from Walker's original. However, a helipad was added above the lantern in 1978, giving the keepers an alternative means of access rather than on wave-tossed and often-delayed boats.

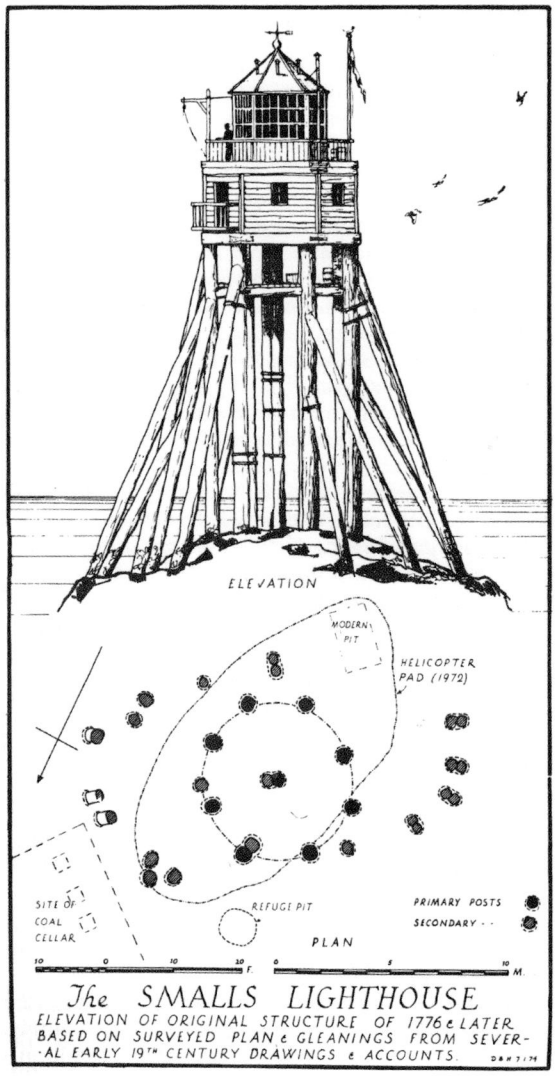

The SMALLS LIGHTHOUSE
ELEVATION OF ORIGINAL STRUCTURE OF 1776 & LATER
BASED ON SURVEYED PLAN & GLEANINGS FROM SEVER-
·AL EARLY 19ᵀᴴ CENTURY DRAWINGS & ACCOUNTS.

Drawing of the first Smalls lighthouse. (Douglas B. Hague)

The 1770s saw the start of the rapid expansion of the port of Liverpool with the opening of George's Dock in 1771. In 1779 the Liverpool dock authorities established a lookout and pilot station on a peninsula near Llaneilian, Anglesey, overlooking Porth yr Ysgaw. Here ships could shelter while the pilots boarded to guide them into the River Mersey. To improve the visibility of the site from sea, two lights were installed in the upper windows of the house in 1781, shining east and west along the coast.

However, its location in the low-lying centre of the peninsula meant that the light could not be seen out to sea towards the north. So, in 1819 the Liverpool dock authorities obtained an Act of Parliament to allow them to build a new lighthouse on the higher ground of the northern tip of the rocky peninsula, Point Lynas. It was many years before the lighthouse was actually erected, but in August 1835 the first light was shown from the new structure. The castle-like, crenulated building was designed by Jesse Hartley, engineer to the Mersey

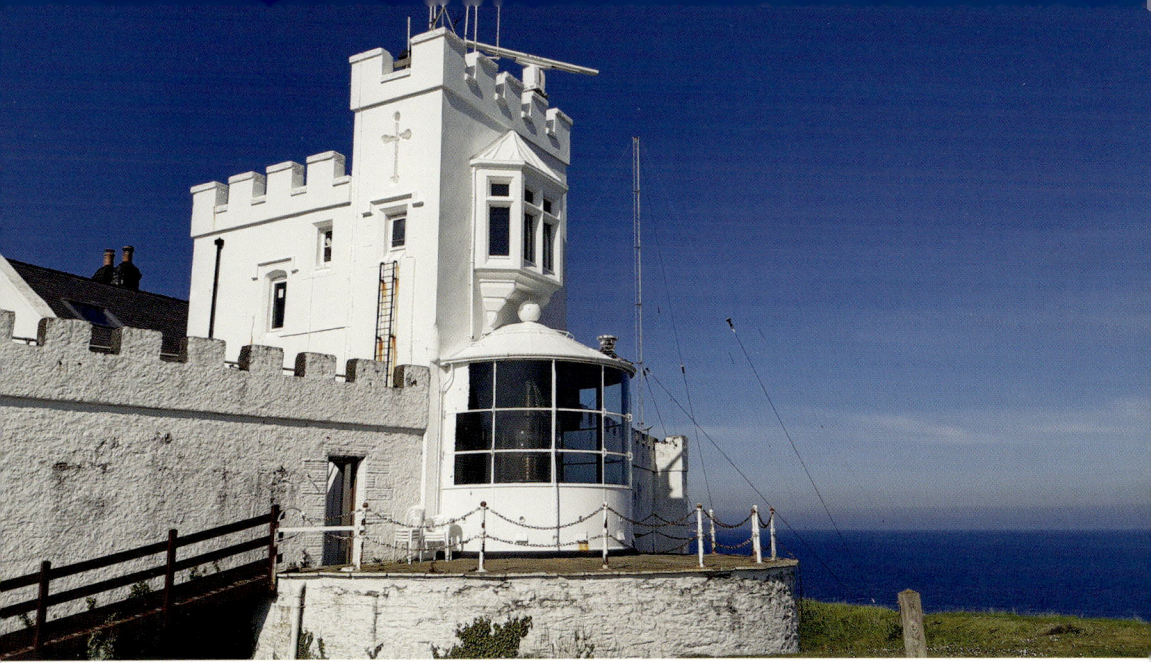

Point Lynas lighthouse.

Docks and Harbour Board. Since the site was already 32 m above sea level there was no need to build a tower. The lantern room is at ground level with a lookout room above. The lantern was enlarged in 1874 and new cottages, boundary walls and entrance archway were added five years later, in a crenulated style similar to the original. The lighthouse was taken over by Trinity House in 1973.

It was another decade before further lighthouses were established in Wales and the 1790s saw three more built. Two of these were part of harbour improvements, adding lights at the end of newly built piers. On Anglesey, shipping out of Amlwch Port had increased dramatically with the growth of the nearby Parys Mountain copper mine, the largest in the world at the time. An Act of Parliament in 1793 led to major improvements to the harbour, including two small octagonal towers at the end of each pier, topped with white lights. The port continued being developed through the nineteenth century, with a new lighthouse built in 1817. In 1853 it was replaced with the current watch tower and lighthouse. This had a light in the upper window of the tower, and was also the base for the local 'hobblers' – boatmen who would watch for incoming ships and row out to guide and tow them in. The light was removed in 1972, and the building is now the home of the GeoMôn geological heritage organisation.

In 1791 the Swansea Harbour Trust was established to oversee the development of the harbour for the city in Glamorganshire. This was also prompted by trade in copper, which was being smelted there, as well as local coal mining and iron production. One part of the plan was a pier along the west side of the entrance to the River Tawe. In 1792 the first light, a lamp on a post, was placed at the location of the planned end of the pier. Once the pier was completed it was replaced in 1803 with a proper lighthouse, an octagonal structure made of cast-iron plates. Initially lit by candles, it was converted to oil lamps in 1845. The light,

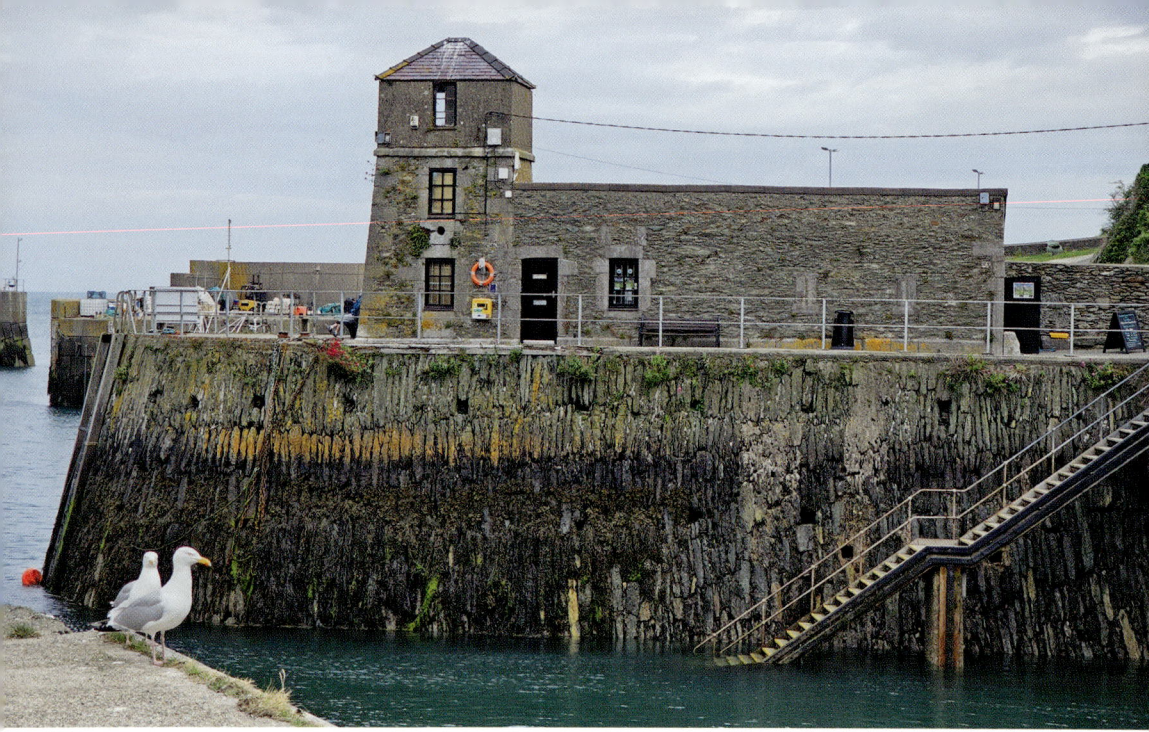

Amlwch Port lighthouse.

coloured red by filters, was only shown at high tides when there was at least 8 ft of water at the entrance to the harbour. During the day a black ball would be raised on a pole to send the same message. The pier was extended in 1878 and the lighthouse moved to the end of the new section. It was again extended in 1909. This time a new lighthouse was built, constructed of timber. This was in use until 1971, when it was replaced with a red light on a concrete pole.

Another part of the plans by the Swansea Harbour Trust was a light on the western approach to Swansea Bay. The Mixon Shoal sandbank and the Cherrystone Rock, 0.8 km offshore from Mumbles Head, posed a substantial danger to shipping, so a lighthouse was planned atop a small tidal island off the headland. Construction started in July 1792, following plans drawn up by the harbour surveyor Mr Molyneux. Unfortunately, just three months later the partially constructed tower collapsed. Molyneux was dismissed and prominent Swansea architect William Jernegan was appointed to form new plans. Jernegan also designed the Swansea Pier lighthouse, and like that the Mumbles tower is octagonal, but made of stone rather than cast iron. The coal-fired light was first shown in 1794. Just four years later it was converted to using an oil lamp, which was enclosed within a new lantern added to the top. In 1860 a gun battery was built alongside the lighthouse to protect Swansea Bay from possible French invasion. The lighthouse was transferred to Trinity House in 1975 and continues operating.

Fifteen years after the lighting of Mumbles Head another iconic lighthouse rose from the rocky islet of Ynys Lawd, off the coast of Holy Island (Ynys Gybi), Anglesey. Located within sight of the Skerries lighthouse, and on the route for ships coming up the Irish Sea towards Liverpool, as well as those from Dublin to Holyhead, this was a particularly busy and

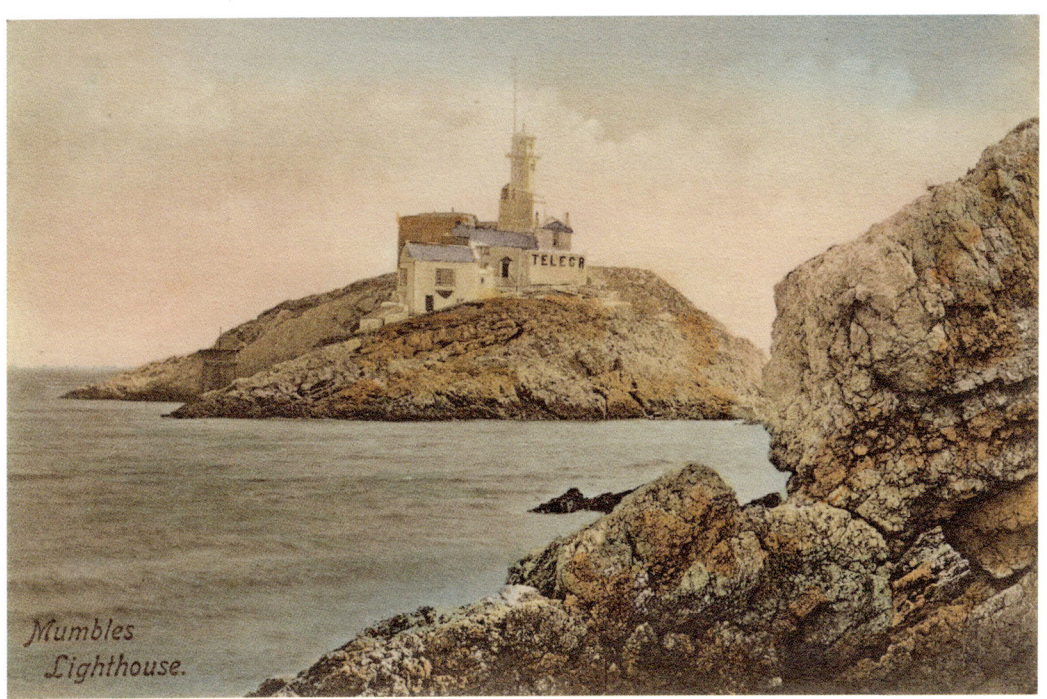

Mumbles lighthouse, *c.* 1893.

dangerous coast. A lighthouse had been proposed for here as far back as 1665, when a petition was sent to King Charles II, to no avail. But in 1808 construction finally began of South Stack lighthouse. The tower was finished in just nine months. It was originally lit by a system of oil lamps and parabolic reflectors, producing flashes as they rotated on a turntable. In 1874 the lantern was rebuilt and a new lighting system, using a lens rather than reflectors, was installed.

Access to the island for construction, and later the keepers, was complicated by the fact that it stood at the bottom of 120-m-high cliffs, on a steep-sided island separated by a chasm through which the sea thunders. But, in addition to a boat landing stage (only usable during relatively calm seas), 400 steps were carved into the cliff face and aerial ropeways strung across the chasm to carry building materials and, later, the workers. After five years this was replaced by a rope suspension bridge, which was followed by an iron one in 1827. It served for 136 years before a new aluminium truss bridge took its place. That in turn was rebuilt in 1996, allowing the island to be reopened to visitors for the first time since it was automated in 1984. It is now the only lighthouse in Wales regularly open to the public, seeing tens of thousands of visitors trooping to the top of the tower each year.

South Stack led the nineteenth-century building boom of lighthouses in Wales. After just a few being built in the eighteenth century, twenty-three new lighthouses were established over the decades of the new century, plus three more in the early twentieth century. Some of the earlier ones were also rebuilt. These later lighthouses will be discussed in the subsequent chapters, as we explore different aspects of the workings of lighthouses and the associated people. The Appendix of this book lists all the lighthouses of Wales and their basic details.

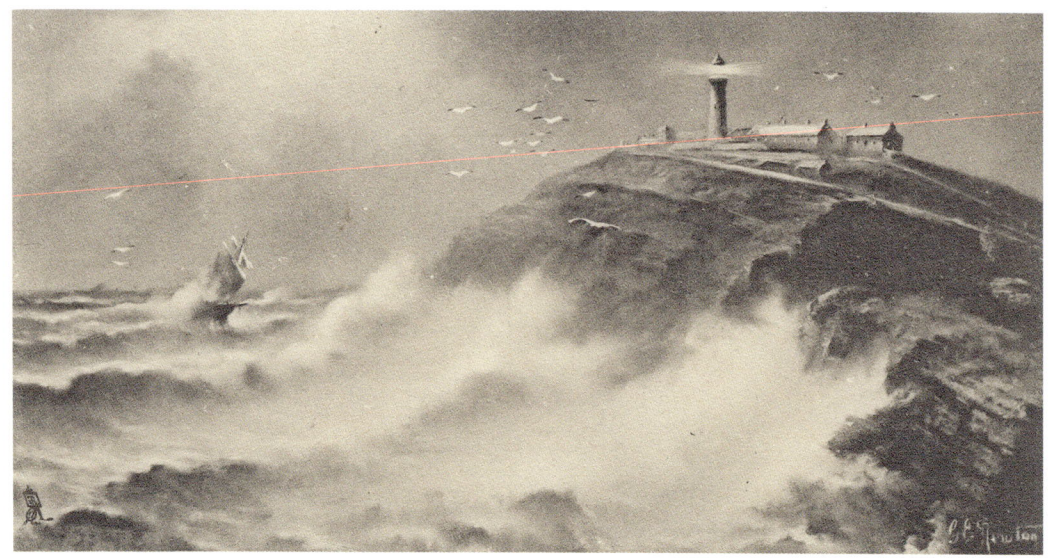

South Stack lighthouse, *c.* 1905. (G. E. Newton)

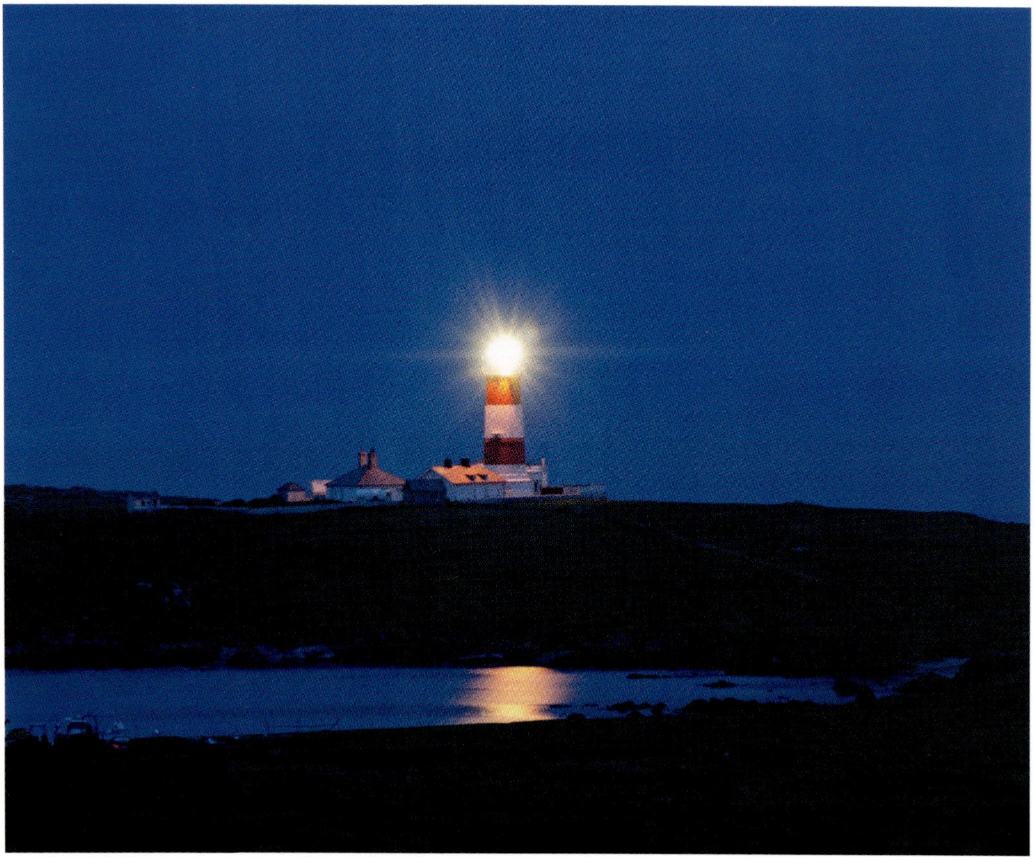

Bardsey lighthouse, built 1821.

CHAPTER 2

Lighthouse Buildings

Lighthouses come in all shapes and sizes, at a variety of locations and for different purposes. Some guide ships in from the deep ocean to landfall, some warn of dangerous reefs, others mark the entrances to harbours. Some stand isolated on rocky islets, others on clifftops or on the shoreline.

The main function of a lighthouse is, of course, to raise a light high enough so that it can be seen from the sea. How high that is depends on the purpose of the light. A light marking the entrance to a harbour doesn't usually need to be seen from very far away, so it can be relatively short and use a less powerful lamp. However, those that are guiding ships towards land or warning of hazardous rocks or shorelines must be seen from much further away. Just using a more powerful lamp isn't sufficient, as the curvature of the earth limits the distance from which it can be seen if it is close to sea level. So, a lighthouse tower must be tall enough to reach beyond the horizon.

But there is such a thing as too tall. South Stack, which shines out at 60 m above sea level, was built on an islet at the foot of cliffs that are twice as high. Why not just build the lighthouse on top of the cliff? During the frequent foggy conditions in the area the cloud base is basically at ground level, and thus would obscure a light on top of the cliff. At South Stack the lamp is often still visible even as the fog spills over the cliff edge.

Tower Construction

The majority of the lighthouses in Wales are typical tall, round towers looking out over the waves. They range in height from the 5- to 10-m squat pepper-pot lighthouses marking the ends of piers, like that at Burry Port, to the majestic 42 m of the Smalls rock light. Some depart from the round design. Bardsey Island, Holyhead Breakwater and Amlwch Port host square towers. Mumbles Head, St Ann's and Skokholm have octagonal towers, while Porthcawl Pier's is hexagonal. Lights that are already on high ground often don't need to be very tall, so some like St Tudwal's and Skokholm just have short towers peeking out above the surrounding buildings. Point Lynas and The Great Orme go further, having the lantern at ground level, shining out over high cliffs, while the residence and lookout rooms rise above them.

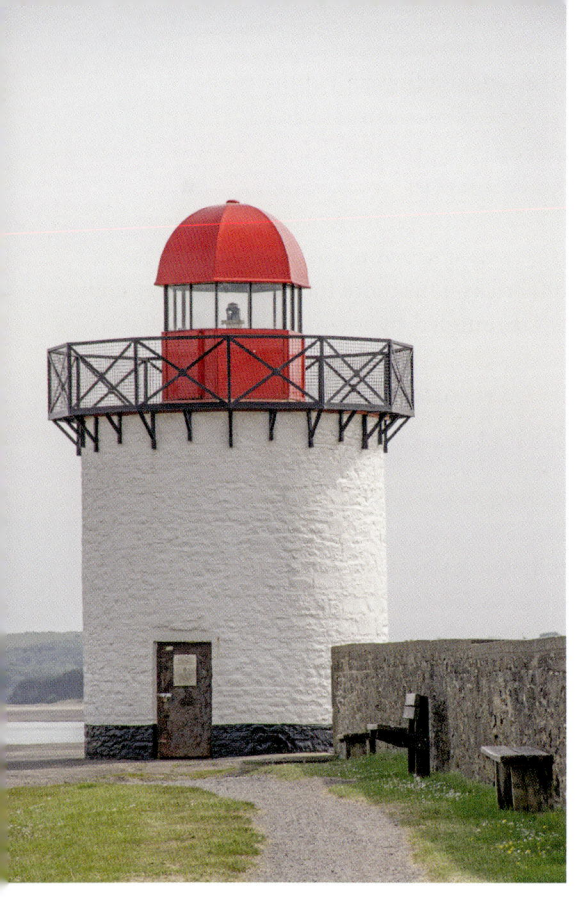

Left: Burry Port pier lighthouse.

Below: The Great Orme lighthouse.

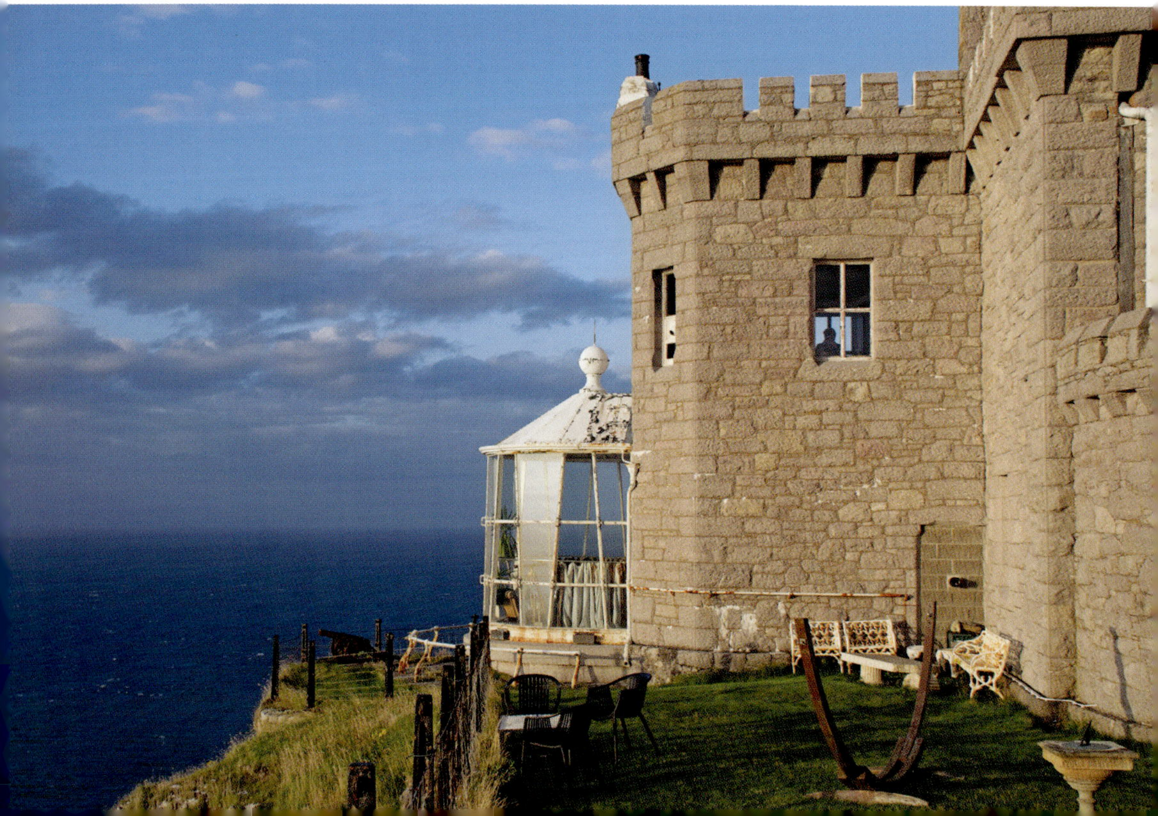

The materials used for building lighthouses vary depending on lighthouse design, local availability of supplies and exposure to the elements. A couple of the Welsh ones are built of easily manufactured and readily transportable brick. The 1815 drawing of the Point of Ayr light, included in Chapter 1, clearly shows the brickwork, although it has since been rendered to give a smooth surface. A builder's estimate for the construction of this lighthouse has survived in the City of Chester archives, showing that the tower required 381 cubic yards of bricks. This is roughly 140,000 bricks, plus more for floors, chimney and stairs. The West Usk lighthouse, a short tower surrounded by a circular accommodation block, is also of made of brick.

Most other Welsh lighthouses were built of stone masonry, usually taken from local sources and reflecting the nearby geology. Many of them, such as South Stack, were built of rough, undressed stone, bonded together with lime mortar and then rendered for a smooth surface. The stone used there was quarried on the island just metres away and a limestone kiln was built nearby to manufacture the mortar. The construction was aided by local masons who were well experienced in building tall structures, having constructed the numerous stone tower windmills that are scattered across Anglesey. The larger lighthouse on Llanddwyn Island, Twr Mawr, was also probably built by them, as it is very similar in shape to the mill towers.

A more expensive and time-consuming, but stronger, method is to use ashlar masonry. With this the stone has been painstakingly dressed into rectangular blocks that fit very closely together, requiring just a thin layer of mortar. In lighthouses, there is an extra challenge in carving the stone to produce a smooth, curved surface, both inside and out. The unrendered bare stone of the lighthouse on Salt Island at Holyhead Port clearly shows the skill that went into the masonry.

The forces of the sea always present a danger to lighthouses. Most of the structures discussed in this book have survived a century or two of storms, although one, the light at the end of the pier at New Quay, was completely washed away in a storm in 1937 and

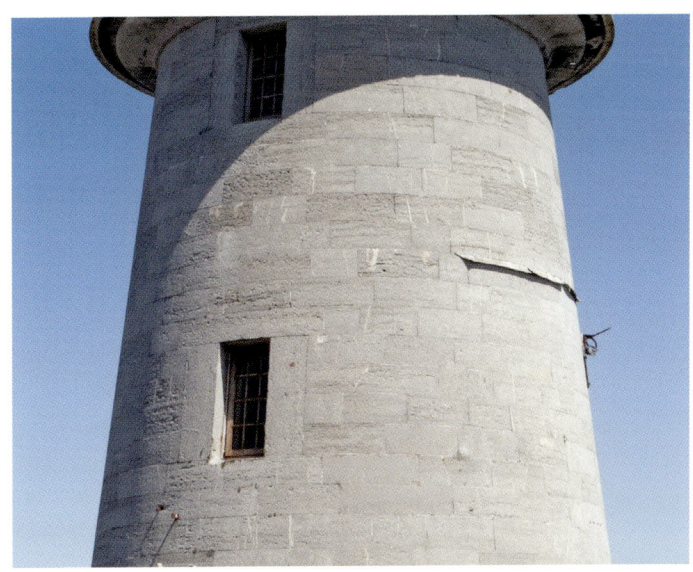

Ashlar masonry at the lighthouse on Holyhead's Admiralty Pier, Salt Island.

never replaced. But the greatest challenge is building a lighthouse on a small, isolated offshore rock exposed to the full fury of the storms. The building of the first lighthouse on the Smalls, a little rock 29 km offshore of Pembrokeshire, was recounted in the previous chapter. It lived alongside the sea by being built on top of timber posts that allowed the waves to pass through, flexing to take the strain of the sea's force. Its replacement followed the new designs developed at other rocks, such as the famous Eddystone, 14 km offshore near Plymouth. The round tower gradually tapering upwards deflects the waves around it and upwards, shifting the force away from directly hitting the walls. It was constructed of the hardest material readily available, granite that was imported from Cornwall. The stones, as well as being cut to precise and tight-fitting surfaces, were individually shaped to dovetail with the neighbours on either side as well as with those above and below. This eliminated any chance of the blocks shifting and causing instability, allowing the tower to stand solid against the sea.

The march of the Industrial Revolution and the development of large-scale cast-iron structures led to the experimentation with building lighthouses from this material. The earliest use in Wales was in 1775 when three cast-iron posts were used alongside timber ones for the piled structure of the Smalls lighthouse. However, in this case the strength of the cast iron proved a disadvantage; they couldn't flex to absorb the power of the waves and they were in danger of breaking or working loose from the rock foundation. They were

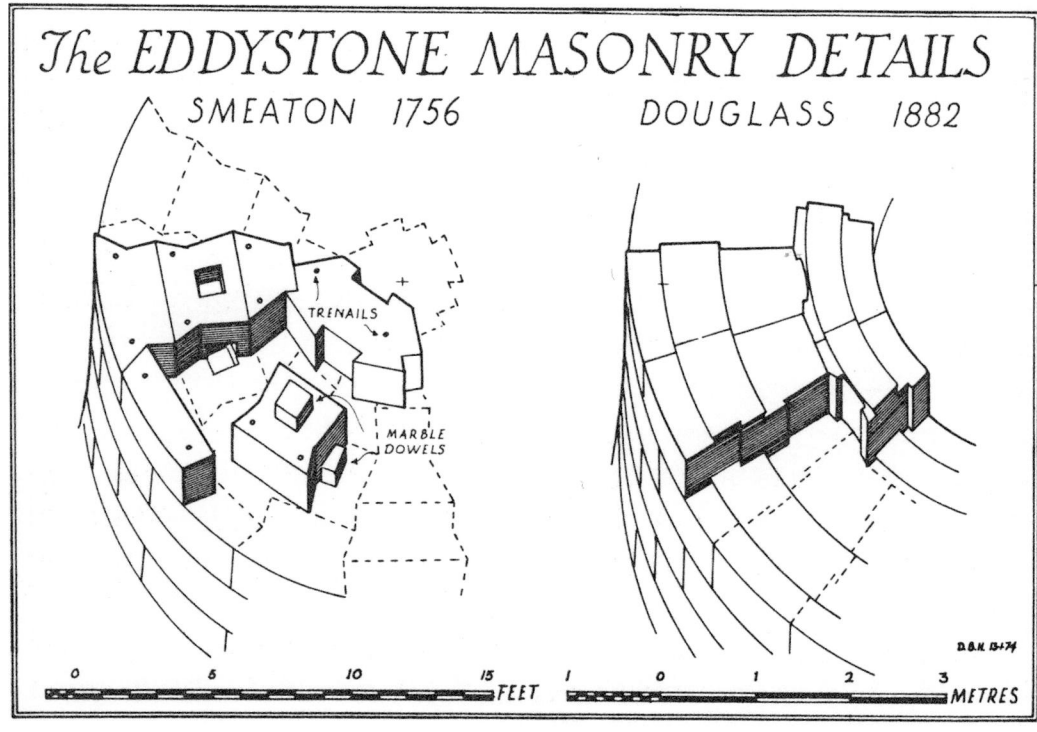

Details of the dovetailed masonry used in the two Eddystone towers, built by John Smeaton and James Douglass. Similar designs were used in later rock towers, including the Smalls. (Douglas B. Hague)

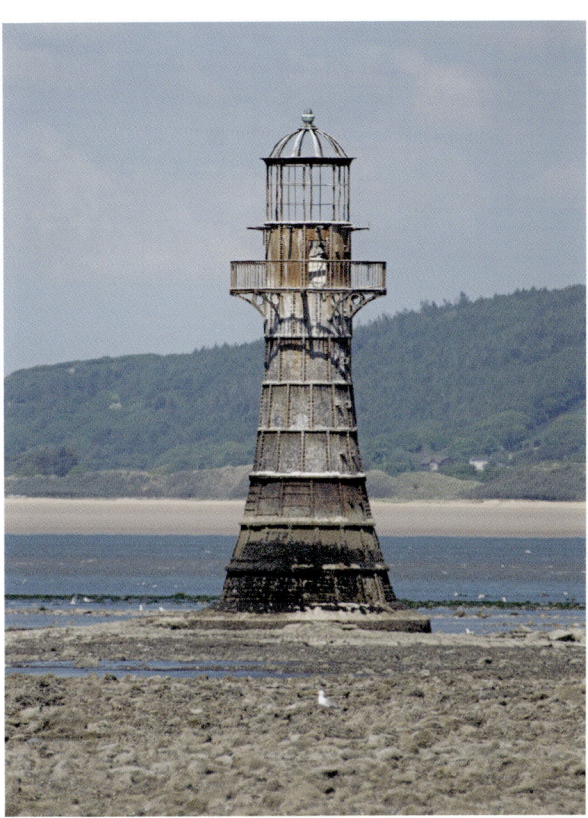

Whiteford Point lighthouse.

eventually replaced with timber posts. In 1803 a lighthouse with a fully cast-iron tower was built on the end of the new Swansea port pier, but this was replaced by an iron lantern atop a wooden platform in 1909 when the pier was extended.

In 1854 another cast-iron lighthouse was built at Whiteford Point, guiding ships into the Burry Estuary to Burry Port and Llanelli. This is an unusual lighthouse because, instead of presenting a smooth surface to the sea, it is made of cast-iron plates rivetted together through external flanges, giving it a very industrial appearance. The fact that it is still standing proudly, after having been abandoned in the early twentieth century, shows how strong the cast iron is. Other iron and steel lighthouse towers in Wales included Burry Port, Porthcawl and East Usk. A cast-iron piled lighthouse structure was built offshore from Point of Ayr in 1844 when that light proved inadequate, but it was replaced by a lightvessel in 1883.

Accommodation

In Britain lighthouse keepers reckoned there were three types of lighthouses, from their point of view of living at them. The first, shore stations (also called land lights), are those that are built on the mainland and can be accessed without crossing water. They will of course be near the sea, often on clifftops or headlands. Most importantly, there will be sizeable accommodation associated with them, so their families could live with them.

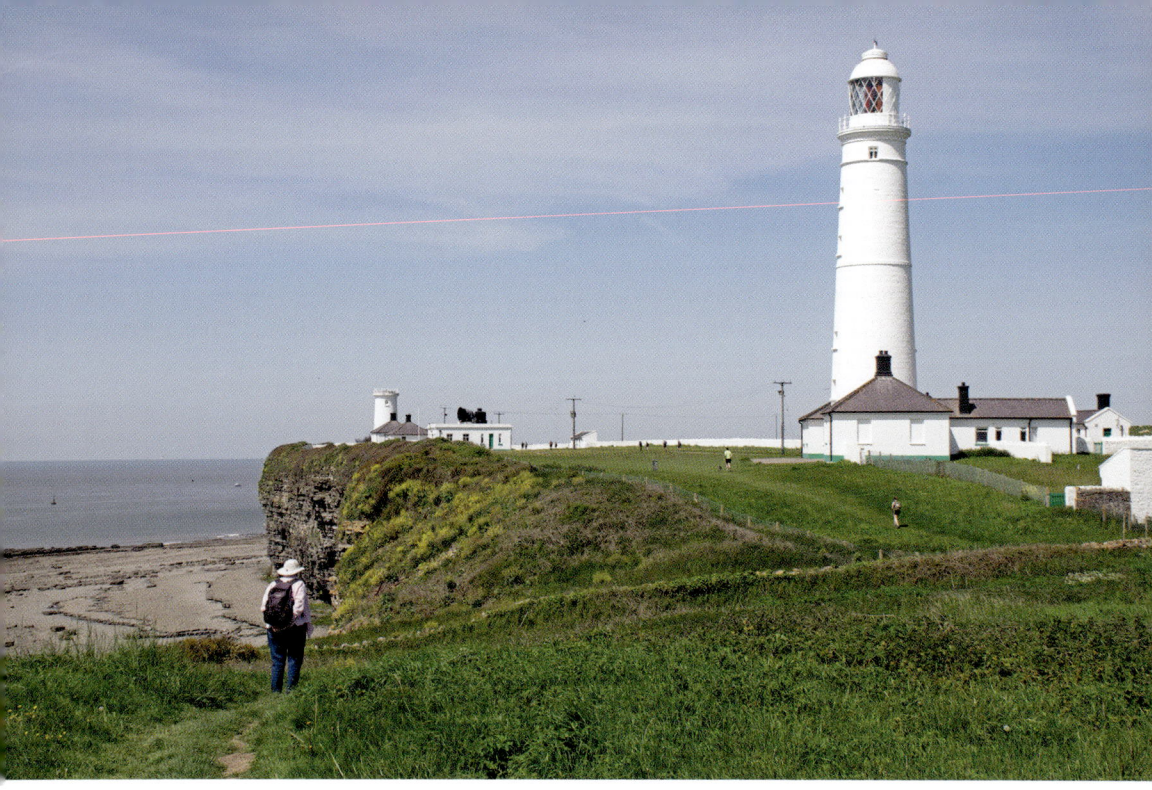

The Nash Point shore station lighthouses, with the family accommodation buildings (now holiday homes).

Access to shops and other amenities was easier, since you didn't have to rely on boats and good weather, but they can still be somewhat isolated and a long way from the nearest town or village.

Rock stations, or rock lights, are those that are built on islands or rocks off the coast. Access to them requires a boat journey (or more recently a helicopter flight), so in general are more isolated. The surrounding buildings included quarters for the keepers themselves, but their families lived on the mainland, usually in accommodation provided by the lighthouse authority. The keepers worked in long shifts. They spent one or two months on duty, keeping a round-the-clock rota that saw at least one of the three keepers awake and minding the light at all times. They then spent a month off the island with their families.

South Stack is one Welsh lighthouse that has spanned this distinction. Although on a rocky island separated by a chasm, there has been a bridge connecting it to the mainland since soon after it was opened in 1809. It was therefore considered an isolated shore station, with accommodation for the families of the keepers, including up to eight children at times. By the early 1930s concern had grown for the safety of the young children on a small island surrounded by sheer cliffs, so it was reclassified as a rock station and the families were moved to the mainland. The same reclassification was previously made at Flat Holm in 1929.

The above two are the types of stations as defined by Trinity House and their Scottish equivalent, the Northern Lighthouse Board. But from a keeper's perspective, there is a third type, the tower light. These are also offshore, accessible only by boat or helicopter, and with limited accommodation space. But in this case the lighthouse is a single tall tower, perched on a small rock or reef just barely above the water (giving them the alternative name of wave-washed rock lights), with no other buildings around it. Once the keepers entered the tower, they were confined to it for the duration of their two-month shift, sleeping, eating and working. There was little chance of having a walk around the island on a nice day or to go for a spot of fishing to supplement the diet (although some tower keepers have been known to simply open the door and cast out their line into the sea below). It may sound like an unpleasant claustrophobic existence, but for some keepers this is a 'proper lighthouse', and they valued their time out there away from the rest of the world, a bit like being in a monastery.

Although there are several famous examples of tower lights around the British coast (such as Eddystone near Plymouth and Bell Rock off east central Scotland), only one was built in Wales. At the Smalls, the original timber structure from 1776 was replaced in 1861 by a tall, graceful stone tower. Inside, a spiral staircase winds its way up through the rooms on successive floors, each serving a different purpose. The lower floors are used for storage of fuel and other items. A sitting room and kitchen occupy floors further up, followed by a bedroom level. Each keeper would sleep in a box bed, curved to fit against the wall of the round tower, giving them the name 'banana bunks'. At the top, just below the lantern room with its lamp and lens, is the watch room or service room. This was occupied by the keeper on watch, who minded the lamp through the night to ensure it was working properly. It also contains control, monitoring and other equipment and has several windows so the keeper could keep watch on the passing ships.

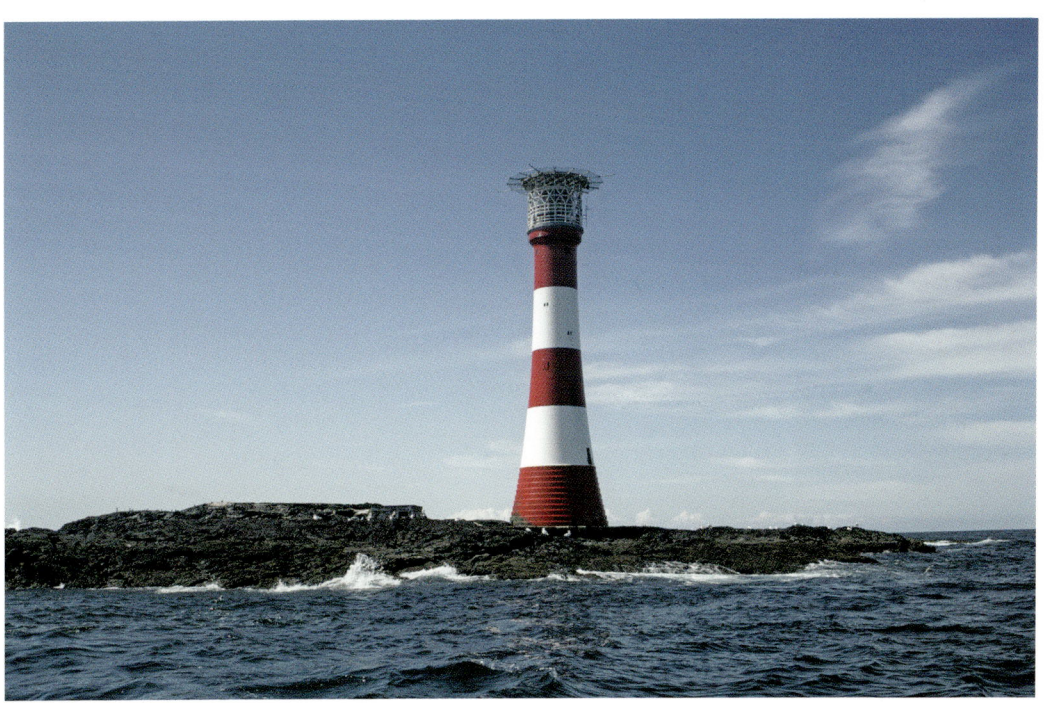

Smalls lighthouse in 2006, before it was repainted all white. (© Crown Copyright: RCAHMW)

The wave-washed tower of the Smalls, standing 42 m high, is the tallest one in Wales. Not only does it have to lift the light high enough above the sea level to be seen at great distance, but it also needs to provide as much room as possible inside for living and storage space. Most others are 30 m or less (with the exception of the equally graceful and 37-m-tall Nash Point light). The majority of them, whether they be land or rock lights, stand in the middle of complexes of other buildings. These will include not only accommodation, but also storage for goods, coal or other fuel, and workspaces. Specialist structures, such as foghorn buildings or telegraph and lookout stations, will often be added.

Bardsey is a good example of a complex of buildings associated with a lighthouse. The compound is perched on the southern tip of a small remote island off the Llŷn peninsula, a place of Christian pilgrimage for centuries and known as the Isle of 20,000 Saints. When first built in 1821 the unusual square tower (the only other ones in Wales are at the Holyhead Breakwater and Amlwch Port) was paired with an adjacent rectangular keepers' accommodation building. The two were connected by a corridor that allowed them to avoid the weather when attending the light. Seven years later a foghorn was erected – a small square building housing equipment to power the horn on the roof. The entire complex was surrounded by a rubble wall that kept the livestock that grazed the rest of the island away from the buildings. It also enclosed a large allotment area where the keepers grew their vegetables and raised pigs and chickens. Later in the century three storehouses were

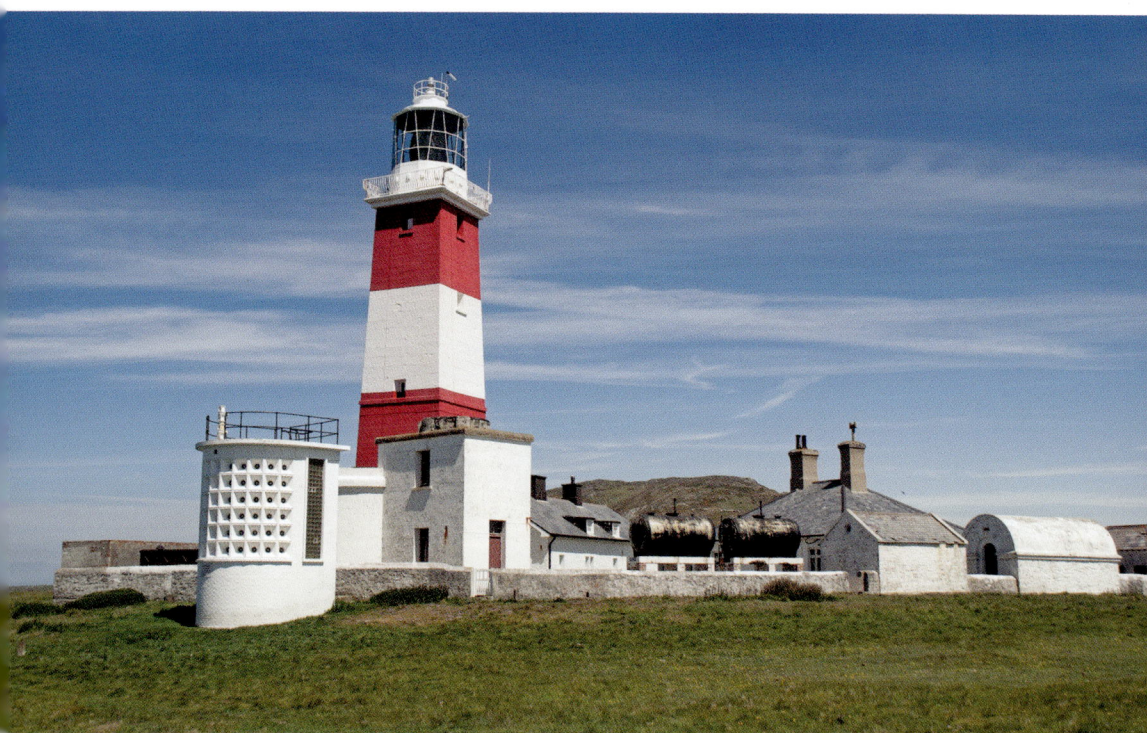

Bardsey Island lighthouse, surrounded by (from left to right) the new semicircular foghorn, circular engine house, square old foghorn building, original accommodation, storage tanks, new accommodation and three storehouses.

built within the compound, including one, with a barrel-vaulted roof, for storing fuel for the light. These were followed by a new, more comfortable keepers' accommodation building and an engine house next to the tower. Finally, in the 1970s, the old foghorn was superseded by a new system of electrically powered horns in a semicircular building just outside the bounding walls.

An unusual arrangement can be found at West Usk, near Newport. Here, rather than having separate buildings, the accompanying quarters are wrapped tightly around the tower in a drum shape, with the lighthouse rising out of the middle. Built in 1821, the first of James Walker's lighthouses designed for Trinity House, it was a simple brick tower 17 m in height. The current dwelling was added sometime before 1861, at a cost of £2,246 (slightly more than the original tower). It was built to house two keepers and their families. When you enter the front door, the spiral staircase ascending the tower appears in front of you. Doorways on either side lead to two accommodation spaces, mirror images of each other, with living rooms, kitchens, sculleries and storage areas, along with stairs leading up to the first-floor sleeping quarters. The lighthouse was decommissioned in 1922 and has since been a public house and inn, private home and B&B, interspersed with periods of dereliction.

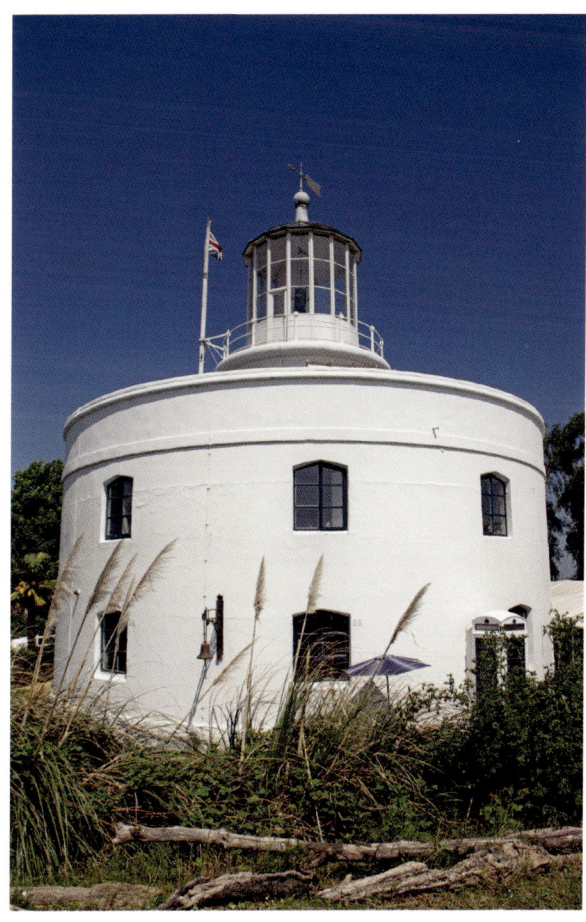

West Usk lighthouse.

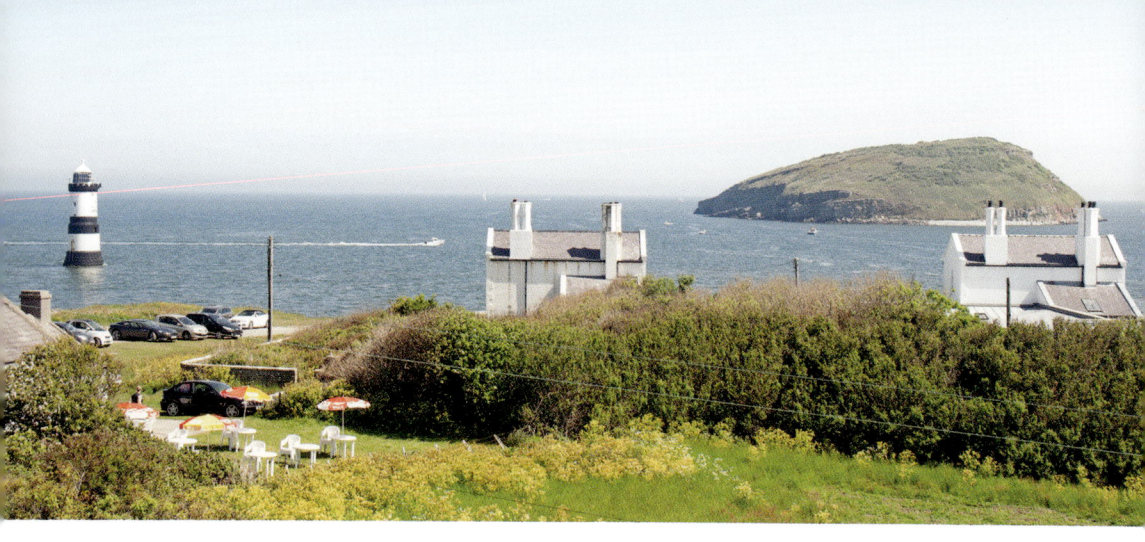

Penmon Point, Anglesey, showing the Trwyn Du lighthouse, two keepers' houses, and Puffin Island/Ynys Seiriol.

Some Welsh lighthouses, for various reasons, have their accommodation buildings a distance from the tower. Trwyn Du, at Penmon Point, Anglesey, is located 200 m offshore. Today it is accessible by foot only at the lowest tides, but in the past the keepers had the luxury of a footbridge that let them reach the tower at all times. Another 100 m inland stands a pair of two-storey cottages that provided comfortable accommodation for the keepers and their families. They were built in 1839, the year after the lighthouse was finished. Also nearby was a lifeboat station and several other cottages for lifeboat crew and pilots, forming a small maritime support community.

At Talacre, the Point of Ayr lighthouse stands on the beach, supported by piles screwed into the sand. Initially the keepers lived in cramped conditions inside the tower. Although a small lean-to extension was added to the tower, erecting any other substantial buildings nearby would require similar foundations. So, by the mid-nineteenth century the keepers were living in cottages that were nestled in the dunes 90 m inland. They continued to be used by keepers when the stone tower was replaced by an offshore piled cast-iron lighthouse, and then by a lightship after 1883, but by 1911 they had begun to fall into disuse. They disappeared sometime in the mid part of the century.

At the other end of North Wales, Llanddwyn Island sports two daymark towers, visible to mariners during the day. One of them, Twr Mawr, showed a light from the window of a small annex at ground level from 1846, until the light was automated and transferred to the top of nearby Twr Bach in the 1970s. The site was also the home of a pilot and lifeboat station, and the crew doubled up as the lighthouse keepers. A terrace of four quaint cottages stands nearby, which housed them and their families, up to nineteen people at one point.

In South Wales another lighthouse was also attended by a part-time keeper. When the small tower at East Usk was built in 1893, a local agricultural labourer was contracted to wind the clockwork that rotated the lamp and clean the glass two to three times a week.

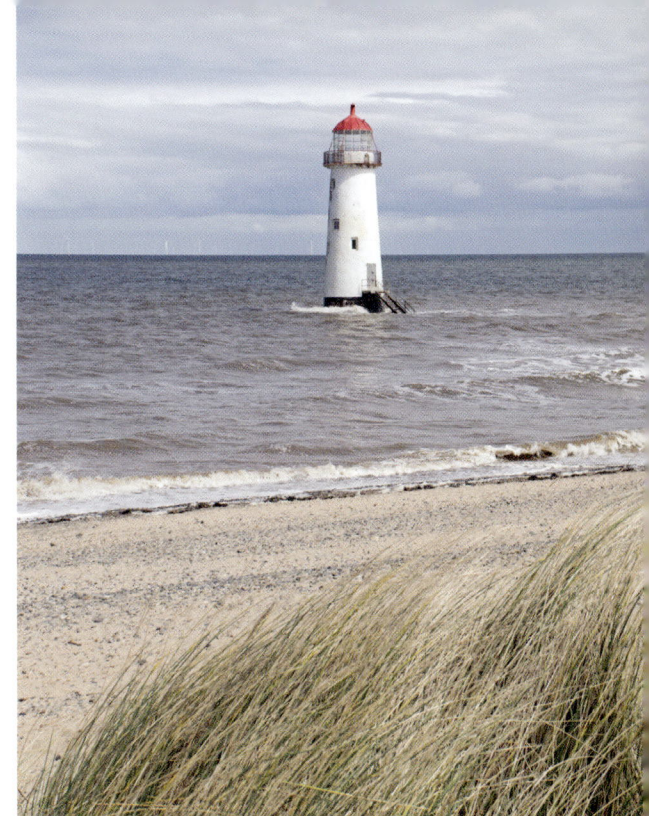

Right: Pont of Ayr lighthouse, Talacre, Flintshire. It is now offshore due to coastal erosion.

Below: Tŵr Mawr lighthouse and pilot cottages, Llanddwyn Island. (Catherine Duigan)

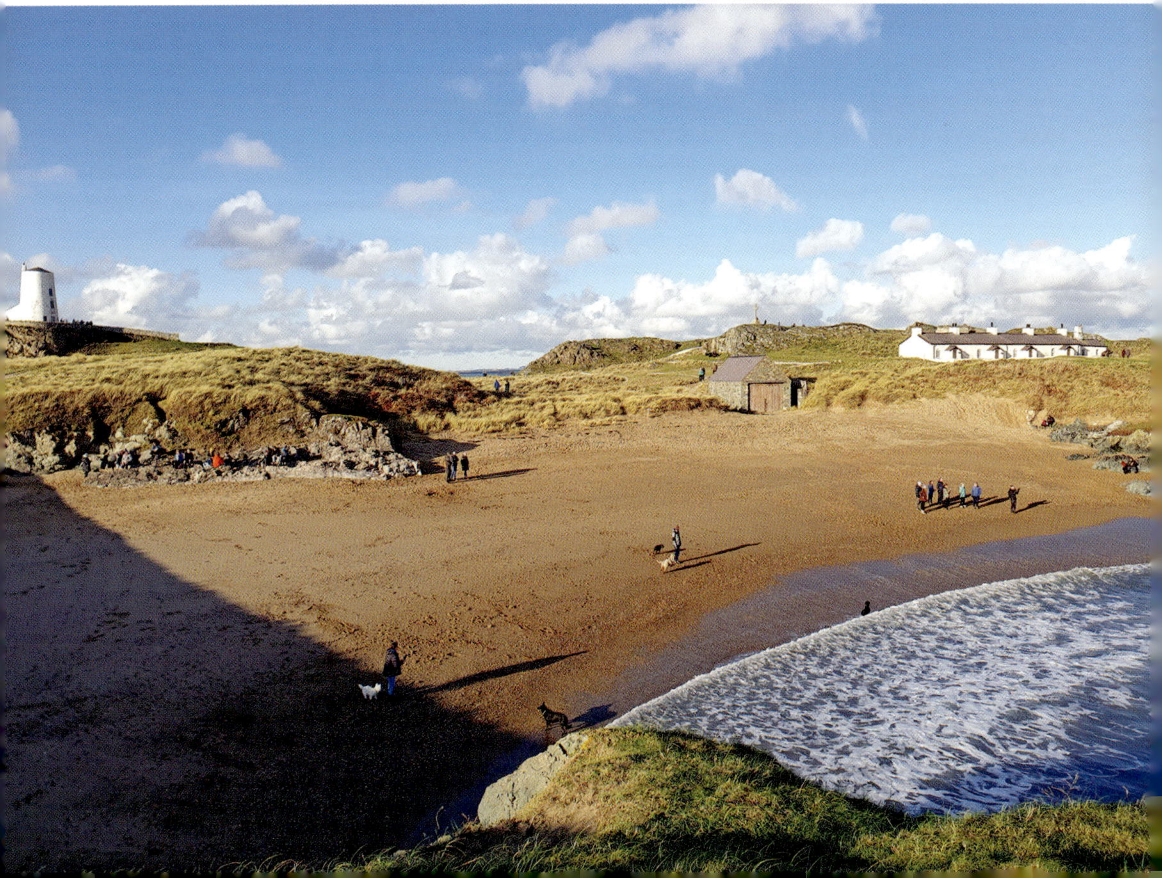

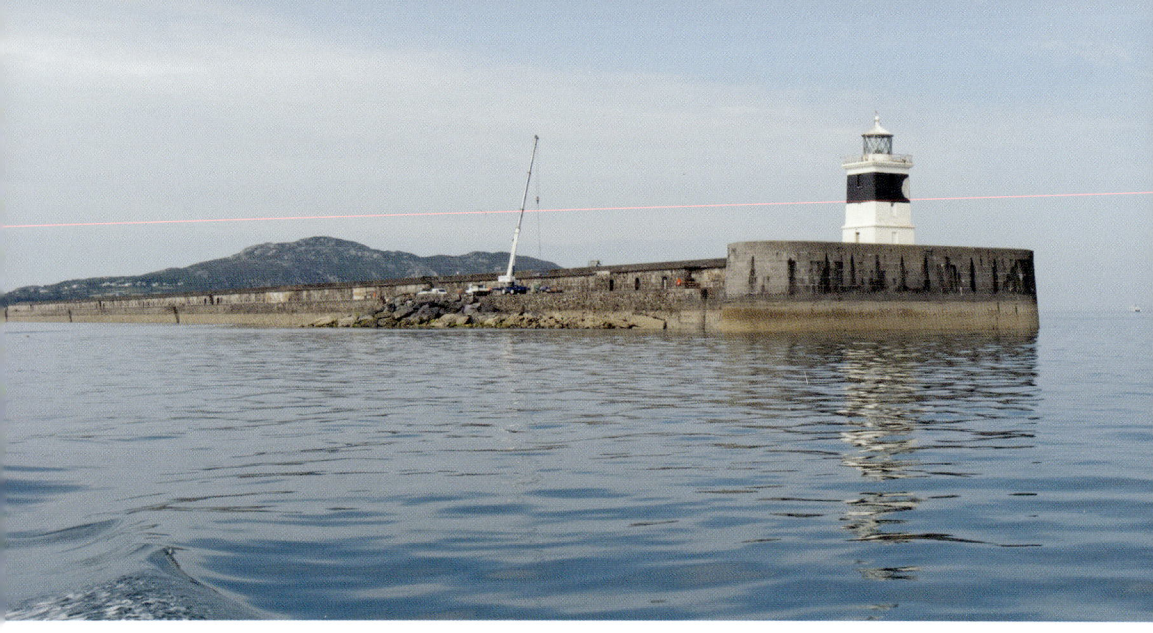

Holyhead Breakwater lighthouse.

He lived in his nearby farmhouse, within sight of the lighthouse, so he could keep an eye on it and make sure it was lit.

Nine of the lighthouses included in this book were built at the end of piers, marking the entrances to harbours. These too were not suitable for having accommodation next to the tower, but ports were the centres of thriving communities, so it was easy for the keepers to walk to the light each day from their houses in the town. The one exception was the Holyhead Breakwater lighthouse. It stands at the end of the longest breakwater in Britain, 2.7 km long, at the far end of the bay from the town. This tower had accommodation for two keepers so that they could stay there while monitoring and maintaining the light. In 1901 the principal keeper, Stanley Blake, was at the tower on census night, with his assistant, Samuel Davis, while their families lived on Cambria Street and Newry Street in Holyhead town centre, 4 km away. Their off-duty colleague, David Williams, was at home with his family in Tower Gardens.

Beacons and Lightvessels

Beacon lights are those that are on various smaller structures rather than being lighthouses that one can walk inside of. They have a greater variety of styles and construction materials than the lights discussed above. Once ships pass St Ann's lighthouse at the entrance to the very busy Milford Haven a number of beacons lead the way through the main channel. Most of these are floating buoys, but several are interesting towers on the shore. Watwick Bay is flanked by two headlands with four concrete towers acting as leading lights. These allow large ships to navigate the narrow channel by lining them up to ensure they are on the right course. Not only do the towers have lights on top, they also have daymarks consisting of slated structures of different shapes. The front three towers on West Blockhouse Point consist of one with a tall rectangular daymark and white lights flanked by two with diamond-shaped ones and red lights, while the single tower 0.8 km away also has a rectangular one. The navigator will align the two rectangular ones while entering the channel.

At the far end of the Haven, at the entrance to Pembroke Dock, a beacon light has found its home atop a nineteenth-century Martello tower. These low, round forts occur around the British and Irish coast and were built to protect against French invasion. Another beacon is located on the domed concrete roof of a water intake structure at Breaksea Point, near Llantwit Major. Further east along the South Wales coast several beacon towers, composed of stone, brick, cast iron or steel truss, mark dangerous points in the Bristol Channel and guide ships into Newport and Port Talbot harbours.

Warning lights are often needed in places where it would be very difficult to build a permanent structure, such as deep water or shifting sandbanks. Today most of these are marked by floating automated buoys, but from as far back as the eighteenth century lightships or lightvessels were employed. These are specially built ships that have a mast in the middle, topped with a lantern. The ships would also have storage areas for lamp fuel and accommodation for the crew, who would stay there for month-long shifts, like the rock lighthouse keepers.

Since they were designed to remain in the same position, most lightships were built with no engines. Instead, they were towed into position by tugs. They also needed to be securely

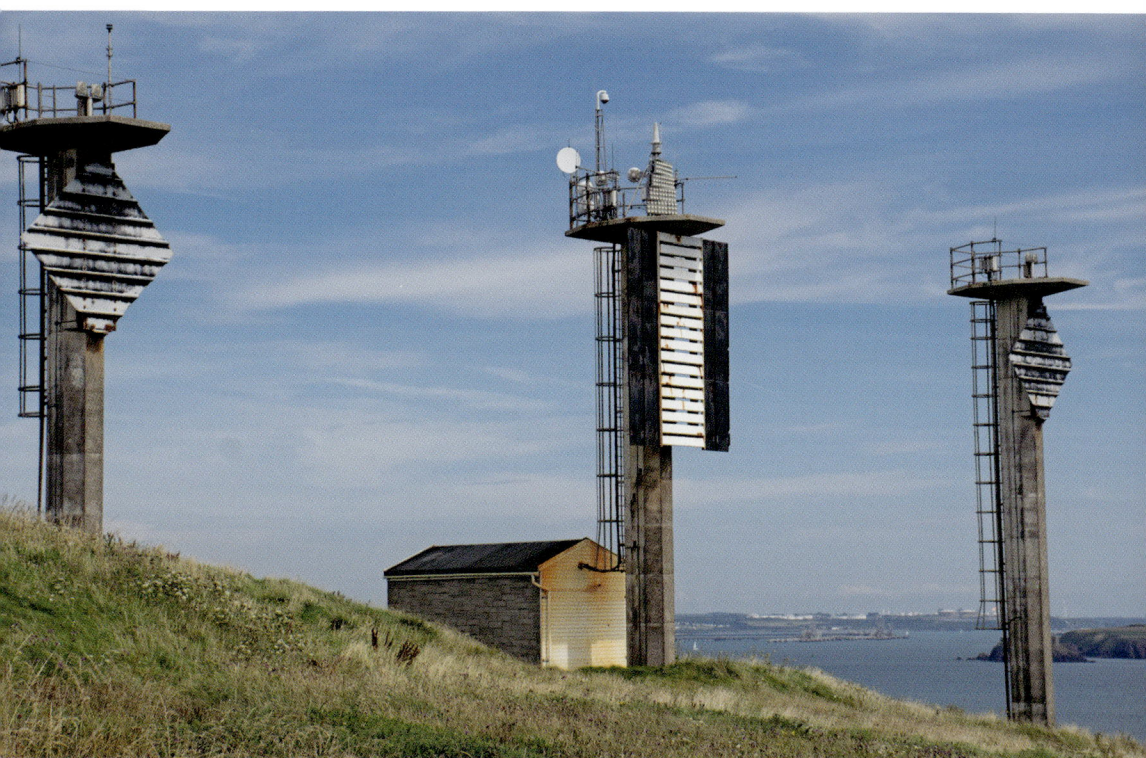

West Blockhouse Point beacons, overlooking the entrance to Milford Haven.

anchored, so mushroom-shaped anchors were used that were less prone to dragging, and spare anchors were ready to be deployed during storms. To enhance their visibility and use for navigation the ships were generally painted red, with the name of the lightship station painted on the side in white letters, as large as possible. Like lighthouses, these would often be enhanced by the addition of foghorns.

As the development of automated buoys progressed through the later twentieth century, lightships were gradually removed from service. Some have become tourist attractions or guest accommodation, others yacht club headquarters, pirate radio stations and sea cadet training ships. A few are sadly rusting away on muddy riverbanks and many more have been scrapped.

Today there are no active lightvessels in Wales, but there are still a few in use around England, mainly in the English Channel. The earliest Welsh vessels were deployed in the Bristol Channel, a wide but hazardous waterway with shifting sandbanks, fierce tides and dangerous rocks. The first lightvessel was placed in 1838 at the English and Welsh Grounds sandbanks, where the deep navigable channel narrows between the two, starting at Cardiff and Weston-super-Mare. This was followed by a ship at the Helwick sands, off the western tip of the Gower Peninsula, in 1846. Others were stationed over the next two decades, with new ones at Breaksea (near Barry), Scarweather (a sandbank near Porthcawl) and finally, in 1907, St Gowan's (off the south Pembrokeshire coast).

In 1859 a lightship was sited in the middle of Cardigan Bay, a wide, sweeping bay enclosed by the tip of the Llŷn Peninsula in the north and St David's Head, Pembrokeshire, 100 km to the south. This was anchored in waters 26 fathoms (47.5 m) deep, so wasn't there to warn of shallow and dangerous conditions. Instead, its purpose was to guide ships through the Irish Sea, clearing Llŷn and Anglesey on the westward side, rather than straying into the bay where the peninsula would block their progress northwards. It lay on the line between

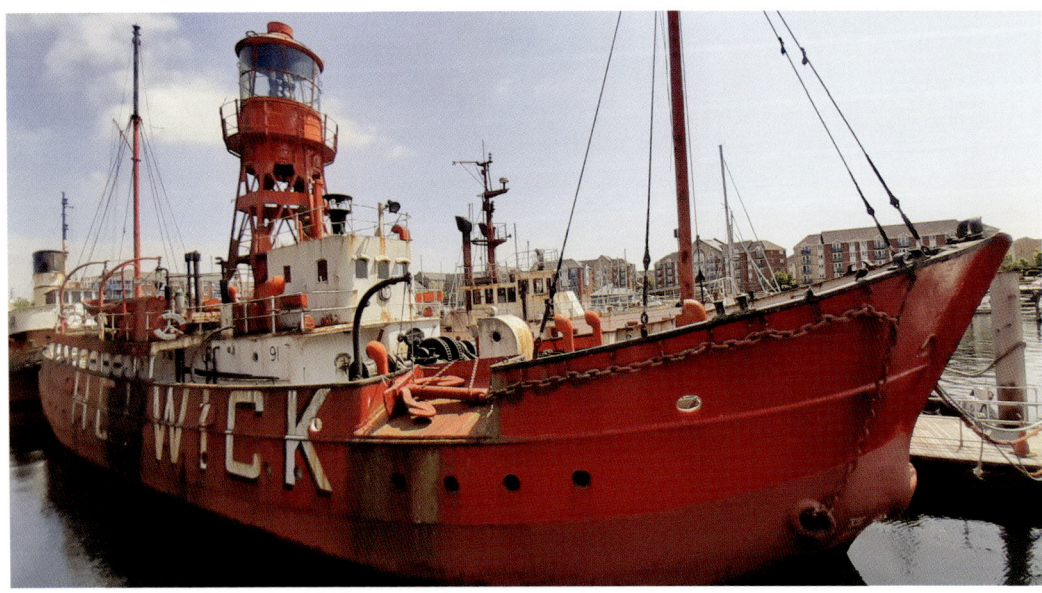

Helwick lightship, docked by the National Waterfront Museum at Swansea Marina.

34

South Bishop and Bardsey lighthouses. In 1869 a lightship was stationed in Caernarfon Bay, 20 km off the coast of Anglesey, to serve a similar purpose. Ships wanting to sail around Anglesey to Liverpool would stay to the west, while those heading into Caernarfon and the Menai Strait would go eastwards. Finally, in 1883, a lightship was placed off the Point of Ayr, on the approaches to Liverpool, replacing the piled lighthouse described earlier. All of these lightships were removed from service in the first quarter of the twentieth century.

Lightvessels used by Trinity House were given numeric designations to identify the ship but also named after the station where they were placed (they were often moved between stations, and thus renamed). The lightship illustrated here, *LV 91*, is now owned by the Swansea Museum and has been docked in Swansea Marina since 1977. She was built in 1937 by the major lightvessel manufacturer Philip & Sons in Dartmouth, and originally served in the Humber Estuary. She finished her working life at the Helwick station, off Gower.

Another former Helwick lightship, *LV 14*, also found a retirement home in Wales, being docked in Cardiff Bay from 1993 to 2015. During this time she was called *Goleulong 2000 Lightship* and was used as a Christian centre. She was sold in 2015 and towed up the Severn River to Newnham, Gloucestershire, where there were plans to turn her into a floating museum. *LV 72* saw service off the coast of Normandy after D-Day in the Second World War, then was stationed in the Bristol Channel at the English and Welsh Grounds. She was retired in 1973 and sold to a scrapyard in Neath. But they had second thoughts about destroying this historic ship and left it on the bank of the River Neath, where it has languished ever since.

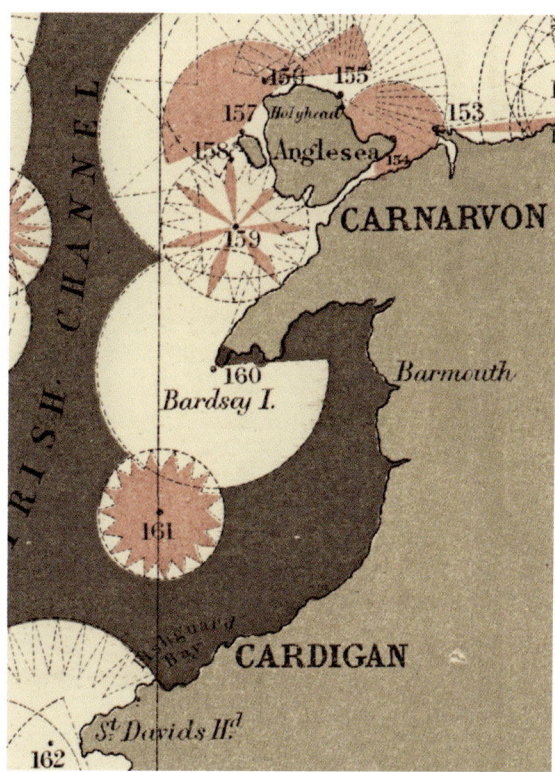

British lighthouse chart of General Coast Lights, 1874, by Woolfield H. F. Hardinge. The Caernarfon and Cardigan Bay lightvessels are numbers *159* and *161* respectively. (National Library of Scotland)

CHAPTER 3

Lamps, Lenses and Fog Signals

Since the day when early humans first sparked a fire into life (probably about 1 million years ago) there has been a march of progress in improving the way that light is produced and controlled. In the context of lighthouses this progression was towards improving the brightness of the light, so it could be seen from greater distances, and decreasing the cost and labour of keeping the light lit.

From the time of the Pharos of Alexandria through the eighteenth century the light in a lighthouse would have come from some type of solid fuel. The most easily accessible type was wood, the cut and dried trunks and branches of trees. However, wood can be bulky

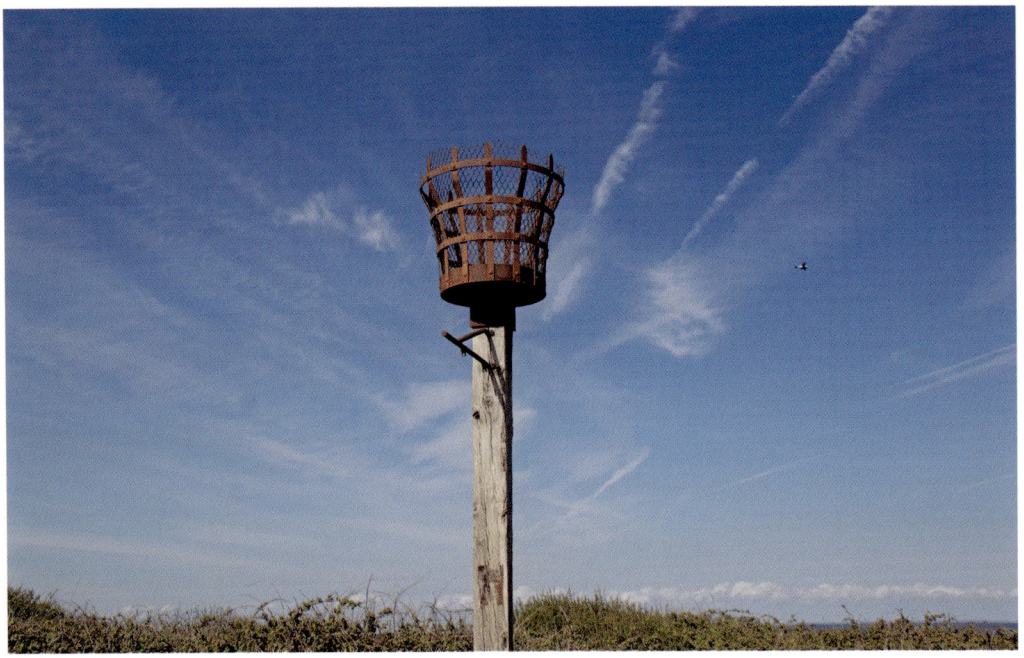

Coal brazier near Hunstanton lighthouse, Norfolk.

and burns quickly, making it labour-intensive to keep stoking the fire. The use of coal was greatly preferred. Formed from wood and other plant material that has been buried in the earth's crust under pressure and heat for millions of years, coal has a much greater energy density. Thus, it burns better and for longer and takes less transportation and storage space.

Sometimes these solid-fuel fires would have burned on a flat surface on top of a tower, but more often they were contained in metal baskets or braziers, allowing air to circulate all around the fire as well as holding it higher up so it was more visible. They generally were open to the elements, which was fine in good weather, but keeping the fire burning brightly in the wind and rain was a challenge. In many situations the light only needed to shine in the seaward direction, so a shielding wall could be built on the landward side, with a roof or canopy over the fire, partially protecting it from rain, but still susceptible to the wind. Attempts to enclose the fire within a glazed lantern usually failed, as the glass would very quickly become covered with soot, despite ingenious methods of ventilating the space.

Coal and Candles

All of the eighteenth-century lighthouses mentioned in Chapter 1 would have started their lives as coal-burning stations. The drawings of these lights in that chapter show the coal braziers on top. The last coal-fired lighthouse to be built in Wales, the Mumbles in 1793, had an interesting arrangement. With open fires there was no way of producing the different flashing patterns that are used today to distinguish lights from others within sight. It was being built in an area where the single light of Flat Holm and the two light towers at St Ann's Head were also visible, so it was desired to do something to distinguish it from the others. This was achieved by building the octagonal tower in a two-tiered manner, so that one fire could be displayed on top and another directly below it on the lower level.

Even with its greater energy density, vast amounts of coal were required to fuel the light. Most of the larger ones would use anywhere from 100–400 tons of coal each year. Carrying coal to the top of a tower up narrow stairs would be very arduous, so cranes and pulleys were often used. Usually these would bring the coal up the outside of the tower, but some like the Mumbles were designed so that the coal could be lifted up the centre of the tower, with the stairs winding their way up the wall around this central space.

Another type of solid fuel was sometimes used in lighthouses. Candles were commonly used for centuries for easily controlled illumination indoors. They were mainly made of beeswax or cheaper animal fats (tallow), although from the nineteenth century the increasing use of petroleum derivatives meant that paraffin wax became more common. The light from a single candle would not be bright enough to be seen from a distance, so when used for navigational purposes an array of numerous candles would be used in a candelabra. Properly maintained by reducing draughts and keeping the wicks trimmed, they did not produce as much soot as coal or wood, so could be enclosed within a lantern, or just shine out from a window facing the desired direction. Even when used in massed ranks in a candelabra, candles would not produce as much light as coal, so were usually used in harbour lights where they did not need to be seen from a great distance. In Wales, candles are known to have been used in Saundersfoot, briefly at Point of Ayr and the now-demolished Swansea West Pier lighthouse.

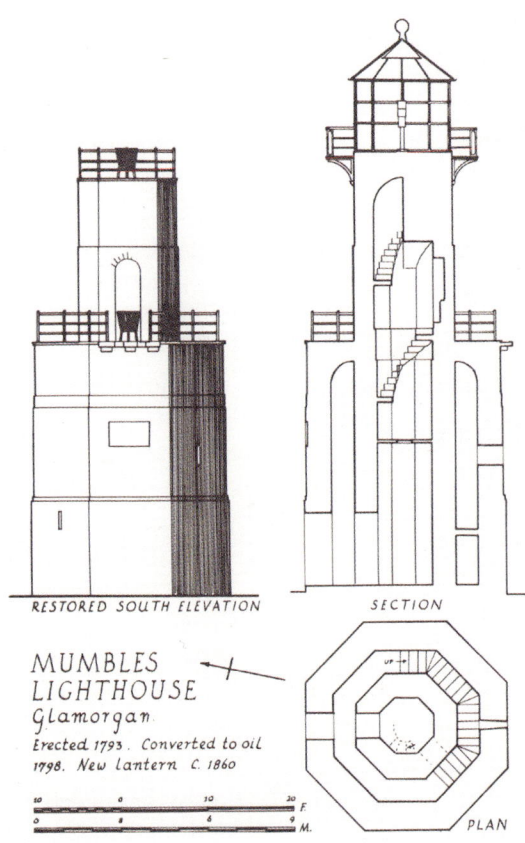

RESTORED SOUTH ELEVATION

SECTION

MUMBLES
LIGHTHOUSE
Glamorgan.
Erected 1793 . Converted to oil
1798 . New lantern C. 1860

PLAN

Left: Drawings of the Mumbles lighthouse, showing the original coal braziers at two levels on the left, and the later design with a lantern on the right. (Douglas B. Hague)

Below: Saundersfoot Harbour lighthouse. The original candle lights were housed in an iron lantern on top, now replaced by a domed roof and electric light.

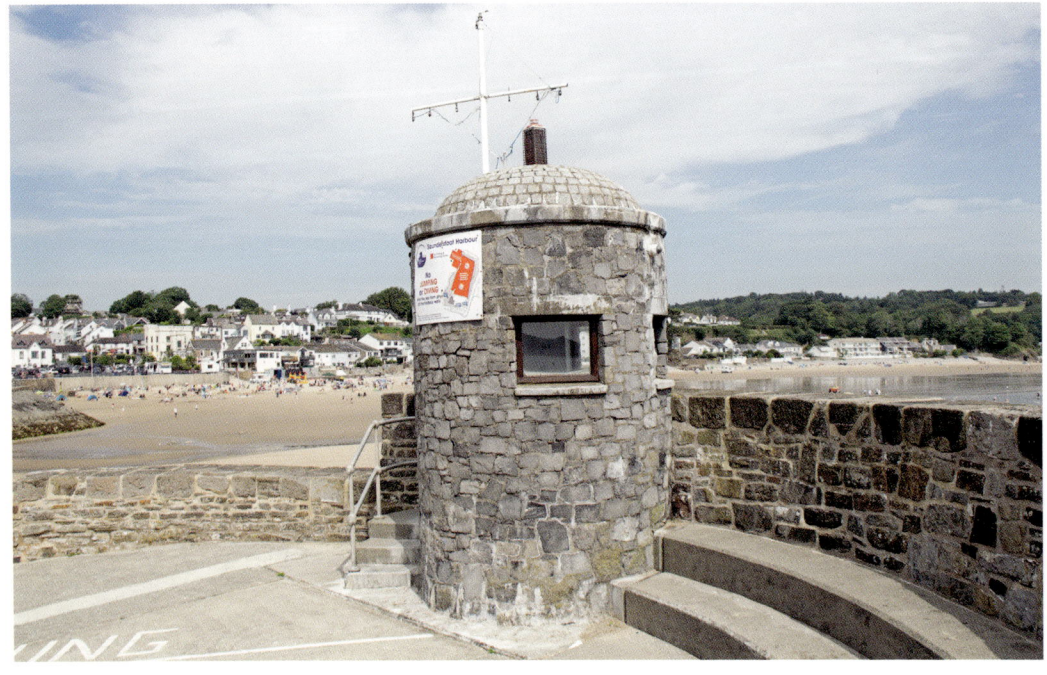

Oil

Oil is another source of light that has been used for millennia. By the Bronze Age oil lamps were common, taking the form of bowls or flat containers that were filled with oil. A groove or hole would be provided that would hold a wick that would draw oil out of the container to the flame. Most oils would be derived from plants, such as olives, sesame seeds or nuts, although animal fats, such as fish oil or dairy fats, could also be used.

One of the earliest known usages of oil for a lighthouse in Britain dates from the fifteenth century at St Michael's Mount in Cornwall. In the southwest corner of the top of the tower of the church is the remains of a small pentagonal tower, with windows on three sides overlooking the approach to the island's harbour. In the centre is a large stone bowl, called a cresset, that would have been filled with oil. A small hole in the centre would have held a wick, which may have been supported vertically by an iron tripod. Local landowner Sir John Arundell's will of 1433 documents his gift of 13 shillings and 4 pence to maintain the light at the church. Other medieval church tower lights, such as the early one at St Ann's Head in Pembrokeshire (discussed in Chapter 1) may have had similar oil lamps. By the time of the building of the first Smalls lighthouse in 1776 oil was increasingly being used instead of coal as the light source for lighthouses.

The type of oil most commonly used in lighthouses in the late eighteenth and early nineteenth centuries was whale oil from sperm whales. This was a particularly bright and clean burning fuel. However, it had the disadvantage of becoming more viscous and slower flowing when cold, so methods had to be devised to keep the oil warm, such as a fireplace in the lantern room, or some sort of heating system under the oil reservoir. By the mid-nineteenth century many had switched to using plant-based rapeseed oil. Not only was this cheaper than whale oil, it was also able to flow more freely at low temperatures. The later nineteenth century saw the rapid development of the petroleum industry, following the drilling of the first major oil well in Pennsylvania, USA, in 1859. Crude oil is refined into various products, including paraffin/kerosene. This was much cheaper and more volatile than the previously used oils and was quickly adopted for use in lighthouses.

Like candles, oil lamps usually use a wick that feeds the combustible liquid up to the flame by capillary action, where it vaporises and burns. The wicks are made from plant fibres, usually cotton, and can either be round threads or flattened strips to produce a wider flame. These would need to be trimmed regularly to remove burnt fabric and shape the top edge to produce an even flame.

A major improvement to oil lamps came in 1780 with an invention by Swiss physicist Aimé Argand. It differed mainly in the design of the wick. Rather than being a solid round or flat piece of fabric, Argand's lamp used a wick formed into a tube. This allowed air to pass up through the middle of the wick as well as around the outside. The flame was also enclosed within a glass tube, acting as a chimney to improve air flow. The combination of the two produced a much brighter flame, with less smoke and reduced the need to trim the wick. Later lamps expanded on this idea, using up to eight concentric wick tubes to produce an even more powerful light.

Another advancement within the Argand lamp was the improved supply of oil. Simply wicking oil up to the flame by capillary action could produce uneven results, with the flame

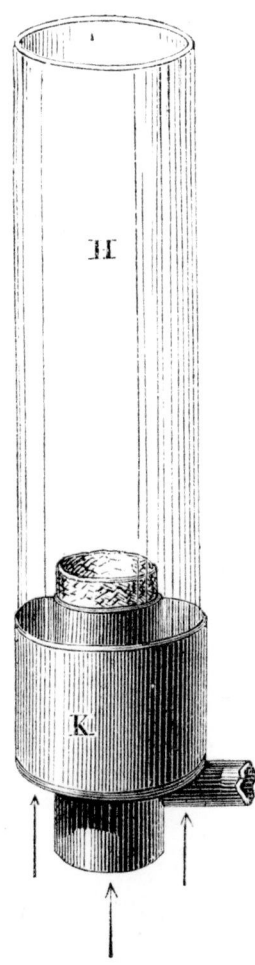

Diagram of an Argand lamp, with arrows indicating the air flow. (From Louis Figuier, *Les Merveilles de la science, 1867–1869*)

becoming dimmer as the oil level in the chamber below went down and the distance the oil had to travel up the wick increased. Argand used a system where a reservoir placed slightly higher than the level of the flame fed oil by gravity to the wick at a constant flow and pressure. Later various systems were developed to mechanically pressurise the oil reservoir to give constant flow without needing a raised reservoir that blocked some of the light and made for a top-heavy system. With the development of petroleum-derived fuels paraffin became widely used in lighthouses. It is more volatile and flows better, so can easily be wicked to a flame, reducing the need for complex pressurisation systems.

In the late nineteenth century lamps using mantles became more common. Rather than deriving all their light from a flame atop a wick, incandescent mantle lamps produce a much larger and brighter source of light. The mantle consists of a loosely woven cloth bag impregnated with various metal oxides. When first exposed to a flame the cloth burns away, leaving a very fragile mesh of metal oxides that glows brightly when heated. When used with paraffin the fuel is vapourised first in a heated chamber, then fed to the burner that heats the mantle.

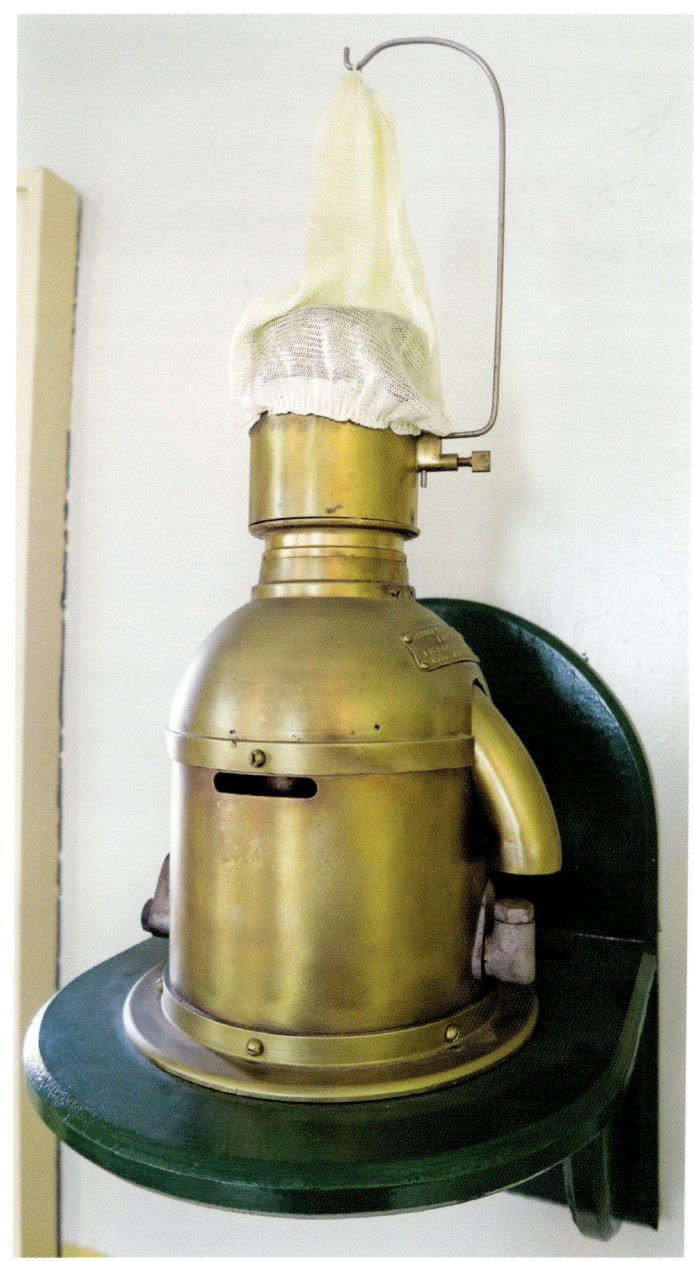

Incandescent petroleum vapour mantle lamp, used at Sumburgh Head lighthouse until 1976. (Wikimedia CC BY-SA 4.0/Etan J. Tal)

Gas

By the early nineteenth century various methods had been developed to produce flammable gas for lighting from various carbonaceous substances, such as wood, peat, coal and oil. One of the earliest uses of gas in Welsh lighthouses was at Holyhead. In his redevelopment and expansion of the harbour in 1821 the well-known Scottish engineer John Rennie built a pier on Salt Island to accommodate the mail ships to Ireland. This was topped with an elegant lighthouse tower, a twin of the one he also built at Howth Harbour near Dublin. The gas that was used in the twenty-one burners in the lantern was produced from oil in gasworks built on the island. This gas also powered the twenty-five streetlamps that lit the pier itself, as well as some of the nearby buildings. The now-demolished lighthouse on Swansea West Pier was also lit by gas, produced from coal.

Gas has the advantage of producing a very bright light, but it was more expensive than oil. It relied on having a large gas-producing structure nearby, which was impractical for many remote lights, particularly rock stations. Also, the technology at the time was prone to producing an uneven flow of gas and thus couldn't guarantee a consistently bright source of light. By 1834, when a major review of lighthouses took place, Swansea had stopped using gas for this reason.

The experience of the inspector for that review when visiting the Holyhead pier lighthouse showed another disadvantage of gas. On arrival he found the roof of the gasometer had been blown off by an explosion the previous day. It was the third such incident since it had been built and one of the workers was killed. The gasometer had been leaking and was supposedly emptied of gas before a repairman approached it with a candle, with fatal results.

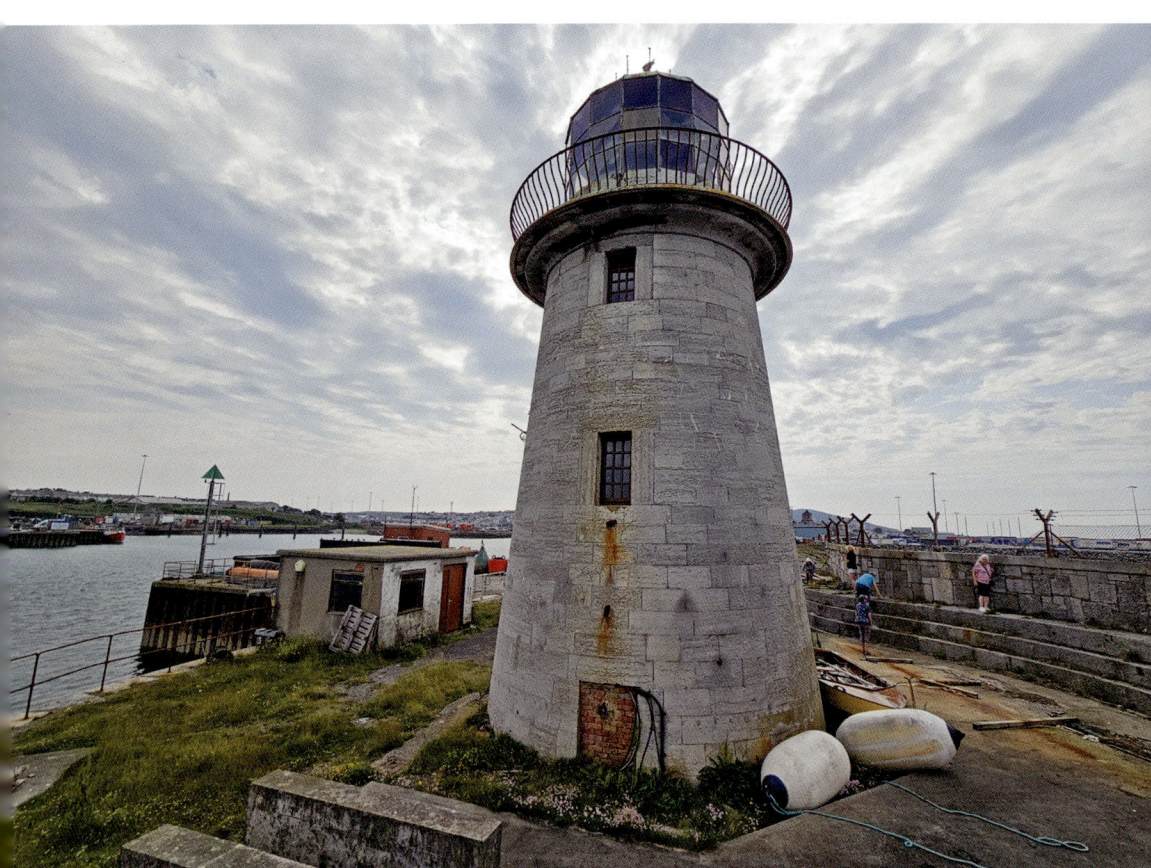

Rennie's lighthouse on Admiralty Pier, Salt Island, Holyhead.

A major advance in the use of gas for lighthouse illumination came with the development of methods to produce the brightly burning acetylene gas. It was first discovered in 1836 by Edmund Davy, but in 1892 Thomas Leopold Willson developed a process to prepare calcium carbide, which reacts with water to produce acetylene gas. The equipment and materials required for this gas production took up far less space than needed for coal or oil gas, so was very suitable for use in remote lighthouses. In fact, the whole process could be contained within the lamp itself, with a water reservoir slowly dripping water onto the calcium carbide to produce gas. Further, methods were developed to store the gas in portable cylinders, dissolved in acetone under pressure.

The flow of acetylene gas was also more easily controlled than oil or coal gas, leading to several automation improvements. Many of these were produced by the Swedish engineer Gustaf Dalén. In 1905 he designed a flasher mechanism for acetylene lamps that was able to cut off the gas supply regularly, then relight the flame from a small pilot light. Not only did this save gas, it also allowed lighthouses and buoys to easily have different patterns of flashing lights, something that could previously only be achieved with large rotating mechanisms. Dalén also invented a method for automatically replacing burnt-out mantles with fresh ones.

Most importantly, in 1907 he developed the Dalén Sun Valve, a device that allowed the lamp to be automatically extinguished when the sun rose, then relit when it got dark. This was effected by having one black rod and three shiny metal rods enclosed in a glass tube. As the black rod was heated by the sun it expanded, cutting off the gas supply. Once the sun went down it would contract, opening the valve. These developments were so important that he was awarded the Nobel Prize in Physics in 1912. Incidentally, later in his career he invented the popular AGA cooker.

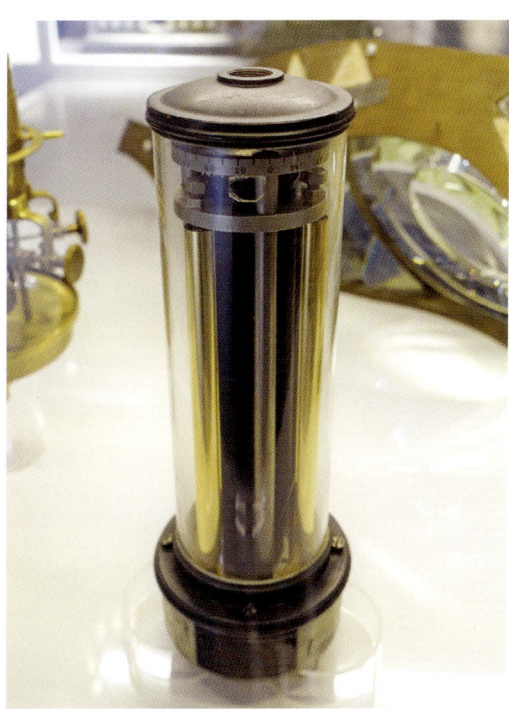

A Dalén Sun Valve, on display at Tekniska Museet, Stockholm, Sweden. (Wikimedia CC0 1.0/Daderot)

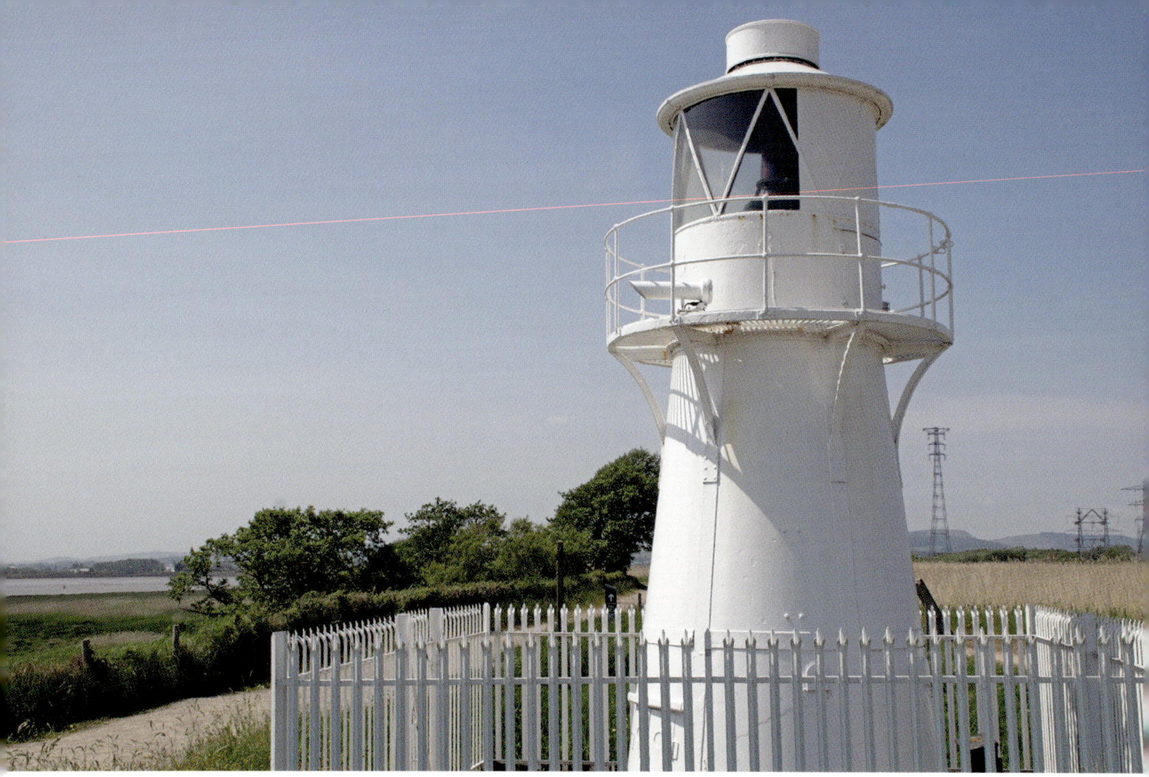

East Usk lighthouse.

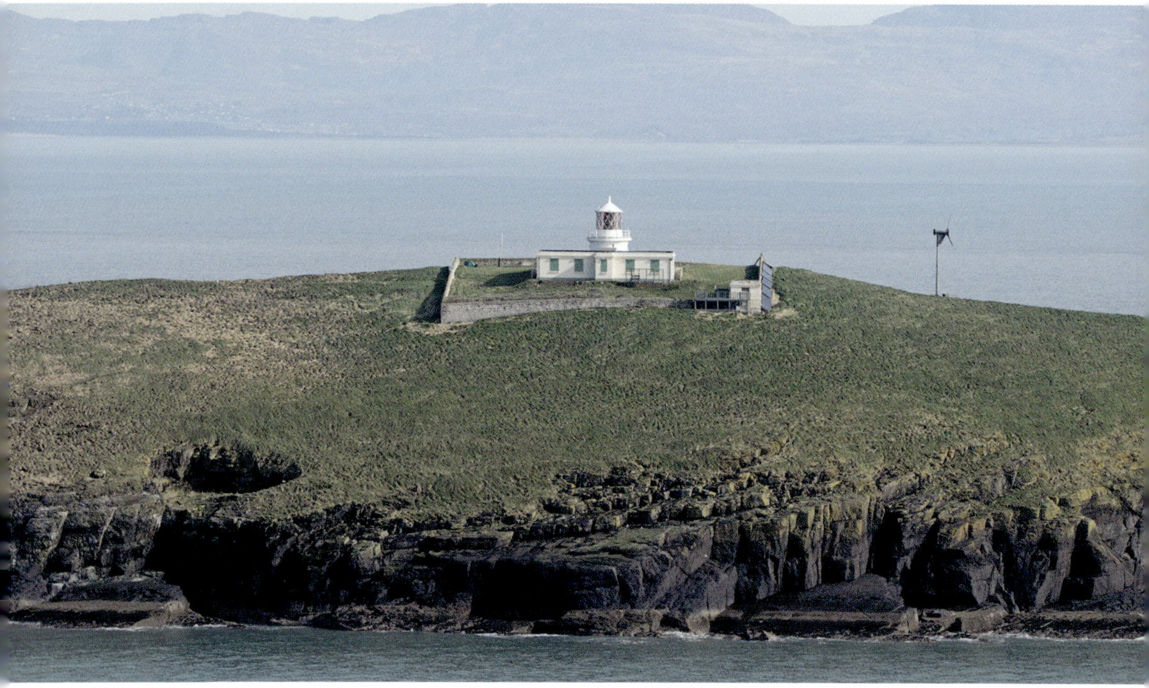

St Tudwal's lighthouse, off the Llŷn Peninsula.

The march of innovations in lighting systems meant that by the twentieth century much of the equipment didn't need constant attention from the lighthouse keepers anymore. This led to automation, where the keepers no longer had to be in attendance full-time, and only visited the lighthouse occasionally for maintenance and resupply. The first automated lighthouse in Wales was the East Usk lighthouse. Guarding the entrance to the River Usk near Newport and first lit in 1893, it was designed to be automated from the start. It was originally fuelled by petroleum gas stored under compression in large tanks that were refilled every four to six weeks. It also had a clockwork mechanism that reduced the flow of gas during the day. In 1917 this was replaced with a Dalén Sun Valve, the first of the Trinity House lighthouses to use the device. In 1919 Whiteford Point was also fitted with one. Trwyn Du and St Tudwal's lighthouses followed soon after, with the installation of acetylene apparatus in 1922. The development of electrical lighting systems accelerated this move to automation.

Electricity

The first step to producing illumination with electricity was achieved by Humphry Davy in the first decade of the nineteenth century. He discovered that an electric current transmitted through two carbon rods with a slight gap between them would produce a spark. Further developments of this phenomenon led to the carbon arc lamp, where a very bright electric arc is produced by ionization of the gases between the two points.

These early arc lamps were powered by electricity produced from chemical batteries. Davy's original battery consisted of an array of 2,000 cells (each with two metal electrodes immersed in a container of liquid electrolyte), which took up a large amount of room and could be depleted rapidly by the large currents required. It wasn't until the invention of the electromagnetic generator by Michael Faraday (Davy's protégé) in 1831 that such lamps were considered for use in lighthouses. In 1836 Faraday was appointed the scientific advisor for Trinity House, a position he held for thirty years. Throughout this time, he experimented with various systems of electrical lighting. He stated that for a safety critical system like a lighthouse the light had to always work perfectly; an unreliable light was worse than no light at all. But he found that most of these systems were not suitable.

In 1853 Frederick Hale Holmes developed an improved arc lamp system. The electricity was produced by a steam-engine-powered electricity generator, and it had a system that would automatically keep the gap between the carbon rods constant (they would slowly be burnt away during use). After extensive testing by Faraday at his workshop at Trinity Bay Wharf, on the Thames in London, the system was installed at South Foreland lighthouse in Kent in 1858. It was also trialled at Dungeness and Souter Point. However, the steam-powered generator required large amounts of costly coal and manpower to keep it running, and they eventually returned to oil-fired lights.

Through the nineteenth century much work was done on developing filament bulbs, where incandescent light was produced by electricity passing through a filament made of carbon or some type of metal. By 1922 the development of reliable filament bulbs and the widespread availability of mains electricity or diesel generators meant that electric power for lighthouses again became feasible, and South Foreland returned to electricity.

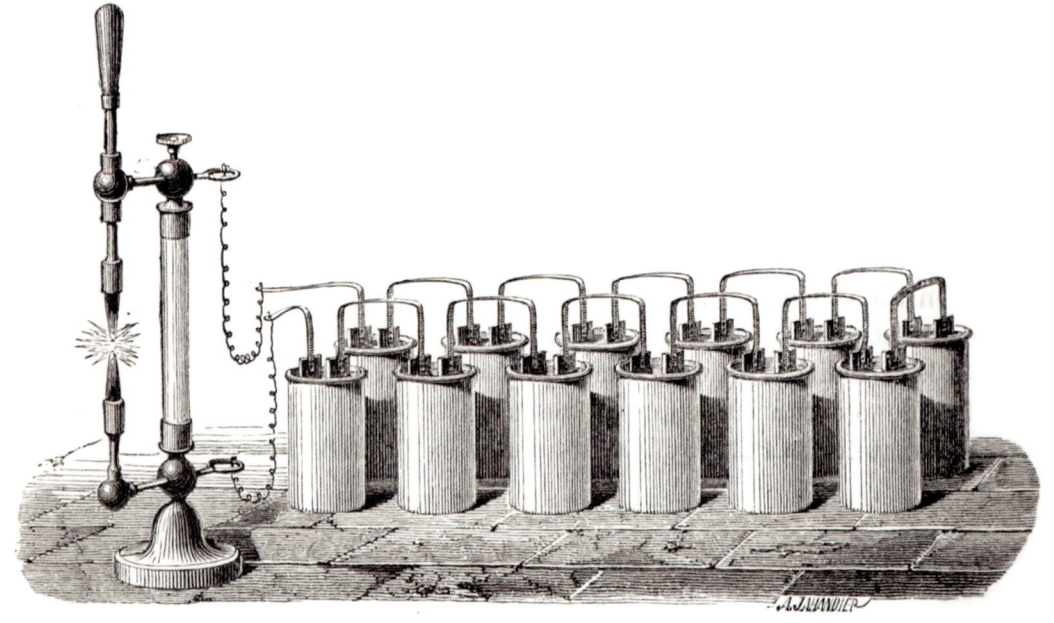

Early experimental carbon arc light powered by a battery of liquid cells. (From Augustin Privat Deschanel, *Elementary Treatise on Natural Philosophy, Part 3: Electricity and Magnetism*, 1878)

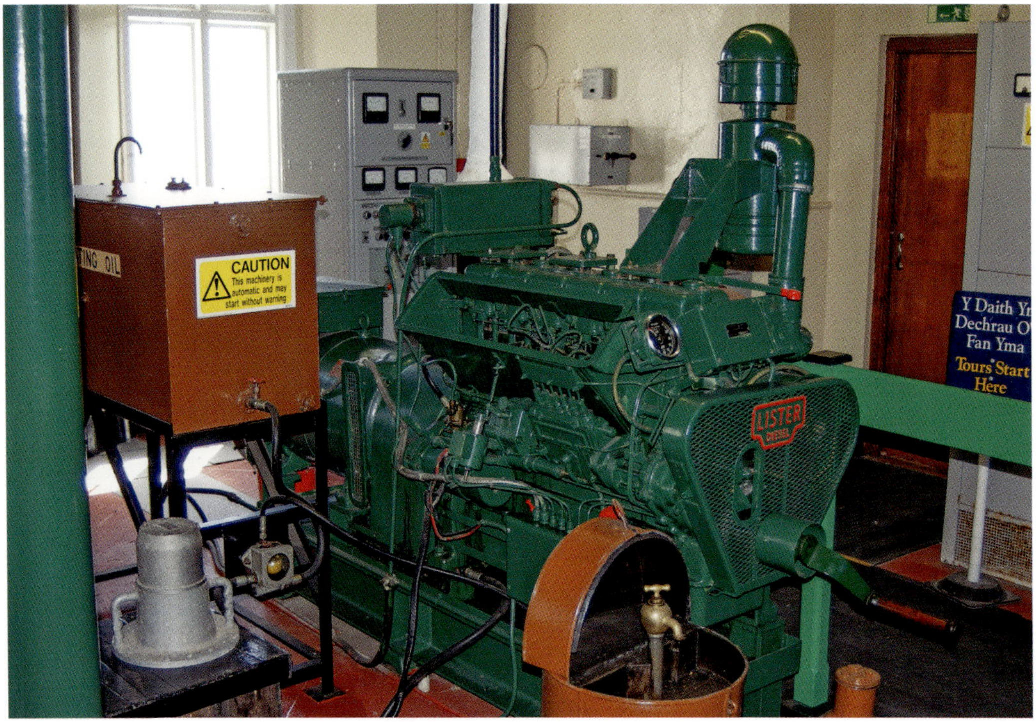

Lister diesel electricity generator at South Stack lighthouse.

The Skerries was probably the first one in Wales to be electrified, in 1927. South Stack followed in 1938, with electrification occurring as part of a major refurbishment. The new electric lamp was rated as being eight times more powerful than the previous paraffin vapour lamp. Electricity was produced by a diesel generator and a series of lead-acid batteries provided backup power. The generator was dedicated to the lighthouse lamp, so the keepers had to persist with other forms of illumination in their quarters until mains electricity was brought to the island in 1963. This was a feat in itself, as electricity poles had to be erected on rocky ground on the very steep slope running down to the footbridge over the chasm, and the poles carried down the 400 steps to the island.

The programme of electrification of lighthouses in Wales was gradually carried out over the next few decades. The last few were converted in the 1990s: St Tudwal's in 1995, Trwyn Du in 1996 and both Caldey and Porthcawl in 1997. The conversion of the first three was planned well in advance by Trinity House, but Porthcawl was electrified out of necessity.

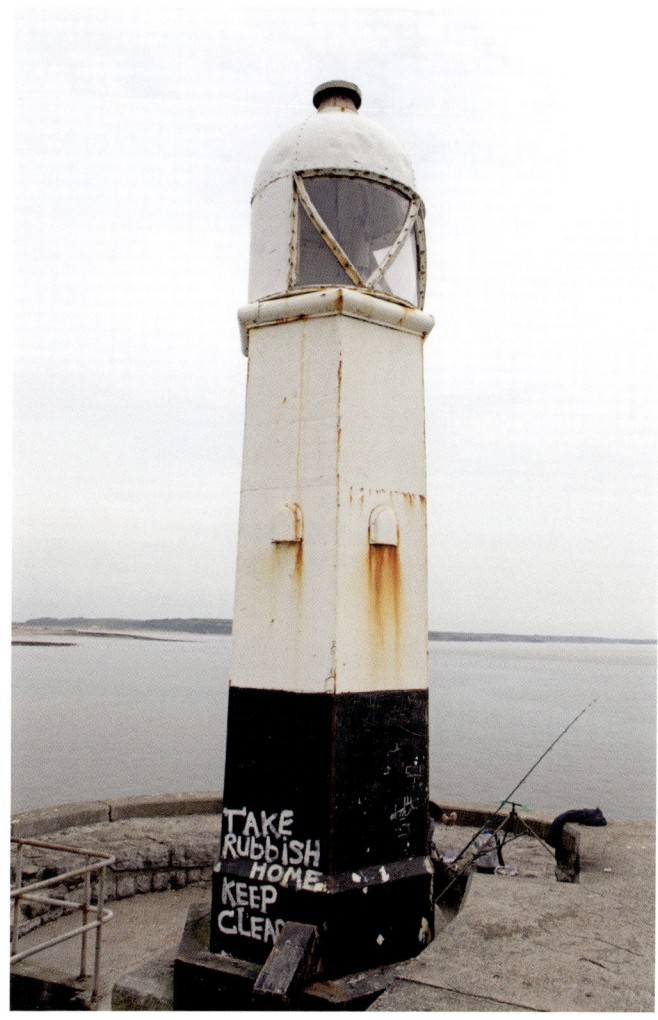

Porthcawl lighthouse.

Waves from a storm the previous year had broken the lantern windows and seriously damaged the gas burner. Replacement parts couldn't be found, so after months of running on a temporary battery-powered light, an insurance payout and listed building consent from Cadw, a new electrical system was installed.

The earliest incandescent filament bulbs used in lighthouses were large, often 30–40 cm tall, with power rated up to 3,500 W. In the 1980s these began to be replaced with mercury vapour gas discharge bulbs. They produced a better, whiter light and used less power, around 400–1,000 W. More modern discharge lamps, such as ceramic metal halide lamps, use around 35–150 W and can be just 10 cm tall.

Light-emitting diodes (LEDs), which could produce light using very little power, were first developed in the 1960s. However, these could only make a deep red light, so were just suitable as indicator lights and in numerical displays. The invention of a blue LED by researchers at the Nichia Corporation in 1994 opened up the possibilities of creating low-power, general-purpose white lights from LEDs; this led to a Nobel Prize in Physics for the inventors.

By around 2009 LED-based bulbs were beginning to be produced to replace standard household and industrial lighting. Lighthouse engineers also saw great advantages in LEDs for their purposes. They use much less power than other electrical lamps, saving money and making solar-powered operation more feasible. Conversion to LED and solar power of lighthouses previously driven by diesel generators can save over £10,000 a year and 15 tonnes of carbon emissions. LEDs also have a much longer life than traditional bulbs (up to ten years). Finally, they can easily be turned on and off, allowing for the different flashing patterns required to distinguish lighthouses. Gas discharge lamps in particular

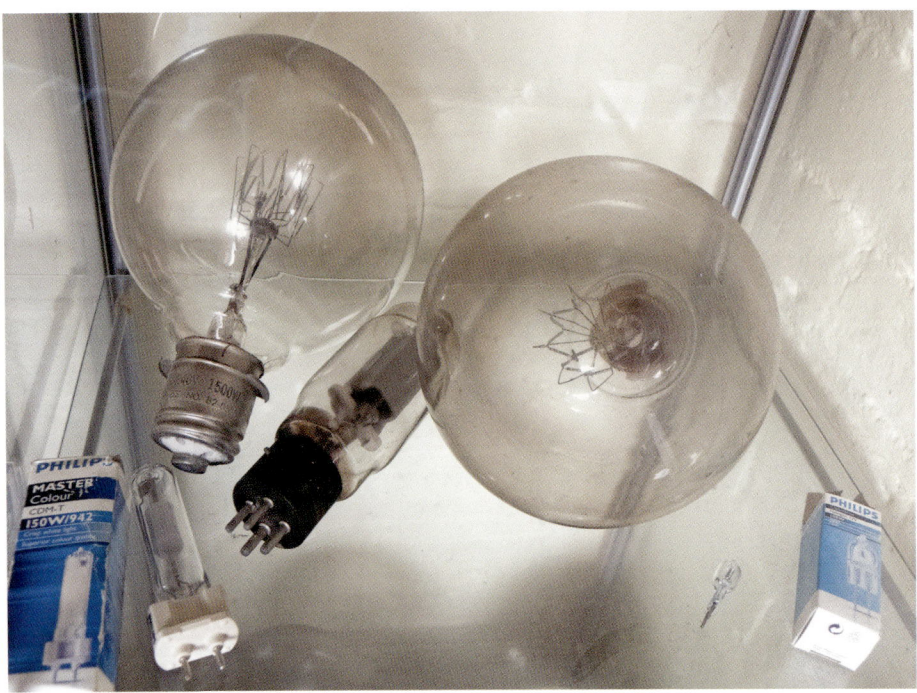

A selection of filament and gas discharge bulbs on display near Flat Holm lighthouse.

take time to get up to full brightness, so cannot produce sharply defined flashes without some mechanism such as a rotating lens or shutter system (see below).

LED lamps consist of small, solid-state devices a few millimetres in diameter. To generate enough light, an array of these diodes is needed. For lighthouses, there are two main types of LED lamps. One type has an integrated lens that focuses light into a plane visible from sea level, often used as emergency beacons or on buoys. The second type features a simple LED array for use within existing Fresnel lenses (see below). Both types include large heat sinks to effectively dissipate heat and extend their lifespan.

Skokholm was one of the first Welsh lighthouses to be converted to LED lighting in 2012. It was followed by Bardsey in 2014. Its new lamp produced a red light rather than the previous white one. This was done because the island is an important stopping point for migratory birds approaching land from the expanses of the Irish Sea. The white light attracted and dazzled the birds, leading to many crashing into the lantern. A number of attempts were made to mitigate this danger, including adding bird perches around the tower and projecting an imitation lighthouse on the ground, but the use of a red light that didn't attract the birds as much resulted in a dramatic reduction in fatalities.

Several other Welsh lighthouses have since been converted to LED, including Trwyn Du, Twr Bach, St Tudwal's, Burry Port, Flat Holm and Mumbles. At the time of writing, work was being done to convert the Skerries lighthouse, and South Stack will follow soon after.

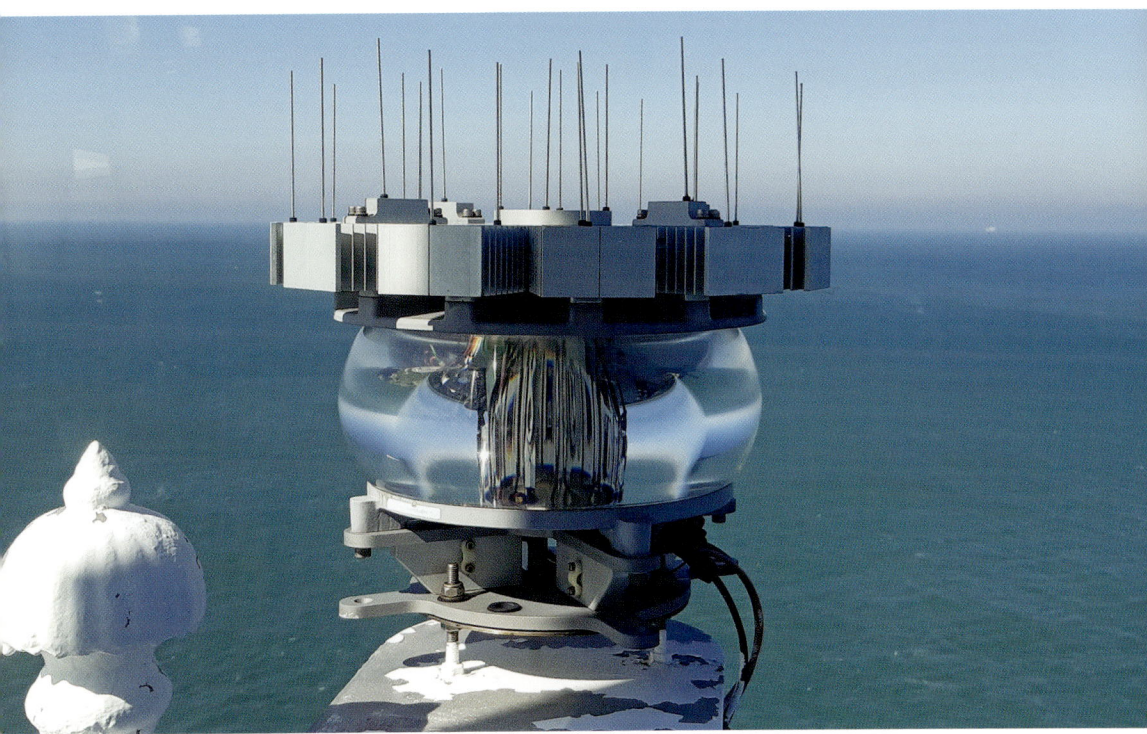

LED emergency beacon at South Stack, with the LED array at the centre of a donut-shaped lens and a heat sink on top.

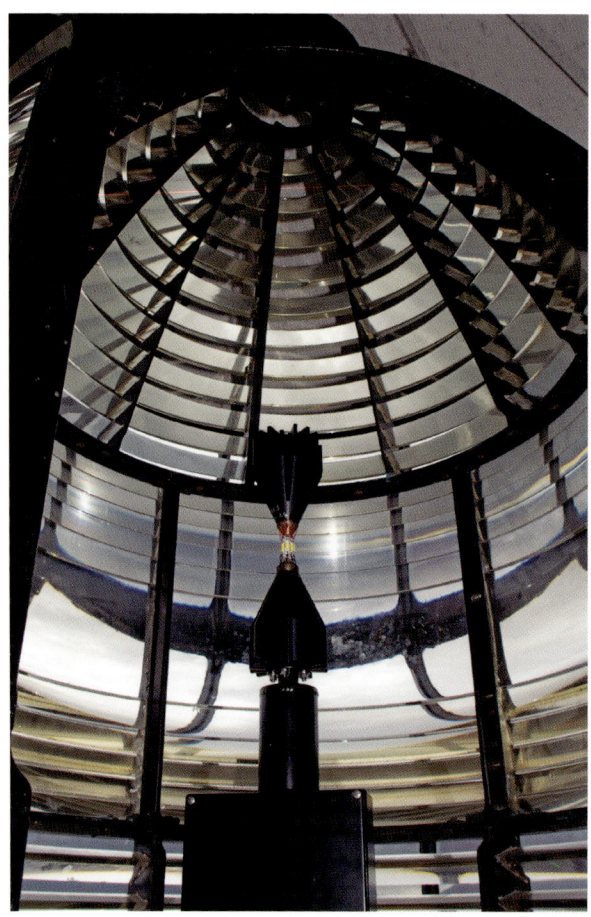

An LED lamp, with heart sink fins above and below the central array of LEDs. It is inside the Fresnel lens at Blacksod lighthouse, Co. Mayo, Ireland. The same type of lamp has been installed at Flat Holm.

Reflectors and Lenses

So far in this chapter we've seen a wide variety of sources of light in lighthouses. All of them produce light that shines out in every direction, left and right, up and down. But usually it is only needed in a certain direction, out to sea, and only at sea level, meaning much of the light is wasted. So, methods were developed to concentrate the light in certain directions, making the lamps more effective.

From the sixteenth century various attempts were made to concentrate light using flat or curved reflectors. The most efficient type, the parabolic reflector, was first devised in 1763 by William Hutchinson, the Dock Master of Liverpool. The paraboloid shape can take light radiating out from a focal point and concentrate it into a beam of parallel light rays. Earlier reflectors were usually polished metal plates, but Hutchinson lined the parabola with pieces of mirror glass, mounted like a Roman mosaic. These were effectively used in several lighthouses on the approach to Liverpool, and similar ones were built by Ezekiel Walker and Thomas Smith for use in England and Scotland, but the large amount of glass in them was heavy, so later reflectors were made of materials such as copper sheets clad with silver.

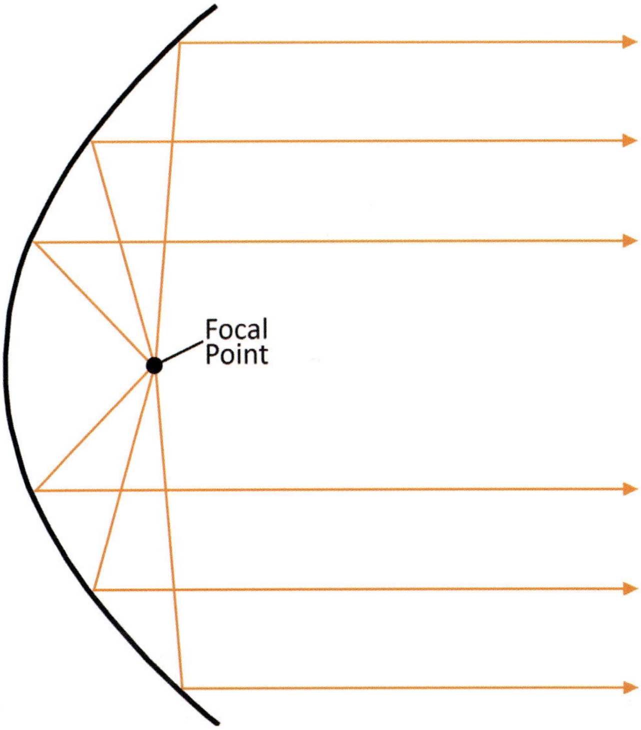

Right: Diagram of a parabolic reflector.

Below: Scale model of a Hutchinson reflector, on display at Leasowe lighthouse, the Wirral. (Wikimedia CC BY-SA 4.0/Phil Nash)

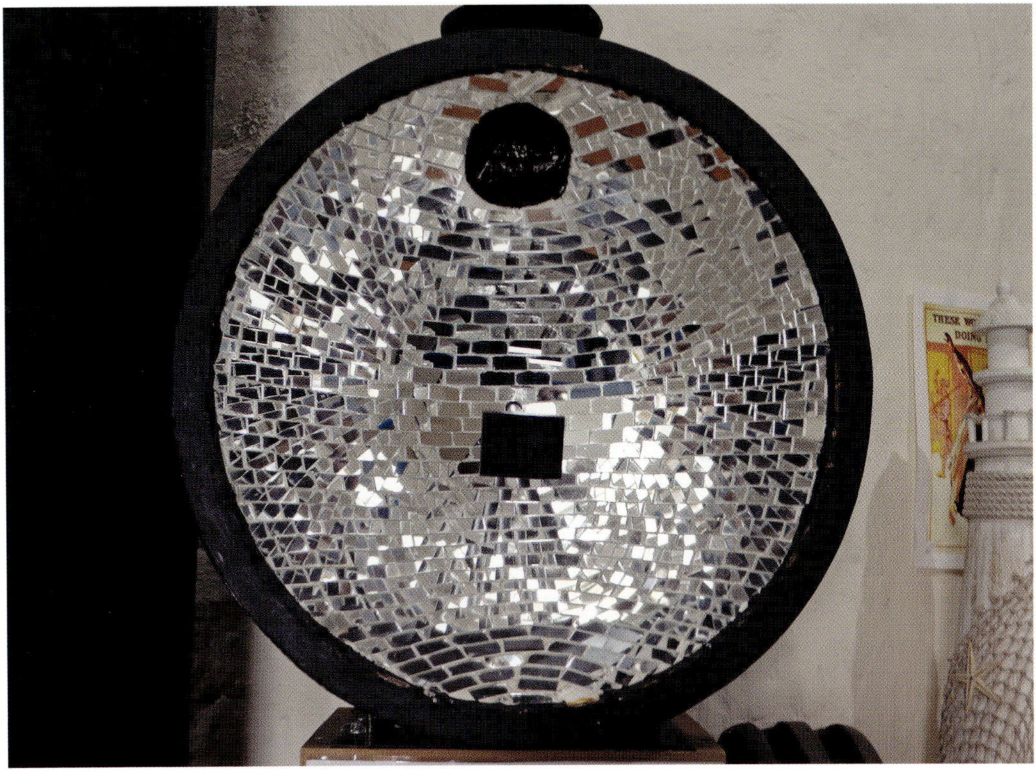

Focal Point

The use of some sort of reflector for a lamp is called a catoptric system. An alternative is a dioptric system, where a lens is used to refract light, bending it into a concentrated beam. From the middle of the eighteenth century attempts were made to use convex glass lenses to magnify the light from a lamp. However, the size of the lenses required meant that it would be very thick in the middle, which would greatly diminish the transmission of the light. The French scientists Count Buffon and Marquis de Condorcet and the Scot Sir David Brewster proposed ideas of reducing the lens into a series of stepped rings that would be much thinner but still refract light. However, technical difficulties meant these were never built. In 1819, initially unaware of this previous work, the Frenchman Augustin Fresnel came up with a design that collapsed a convex lens into a series of rings that had surfaces at the same angle as that of the full lens and thus refracted the light in a similar way. He teamed up with the optical instrument maker François Soleil, who manufactured the glass.

This worked well to focus light into a beam, but there was still a large amount of light that shone above and below the lens. Fresnel initially used flat, polished mirrors flanking the lens to reflect that light forward. He later replaced these with a system of prisms that, through both refraction and internal reflection, more effectively directed the light alongside the main beam. This combination of both refracting and reflecting elements is called a catadioptric system and the whole construction is called an optic.

The Fresnel lens (pronounced 'fray-NEL') revolutionised lighthouse lighting systems. It is often called the invention that saved a million ships and is still in use in numerous

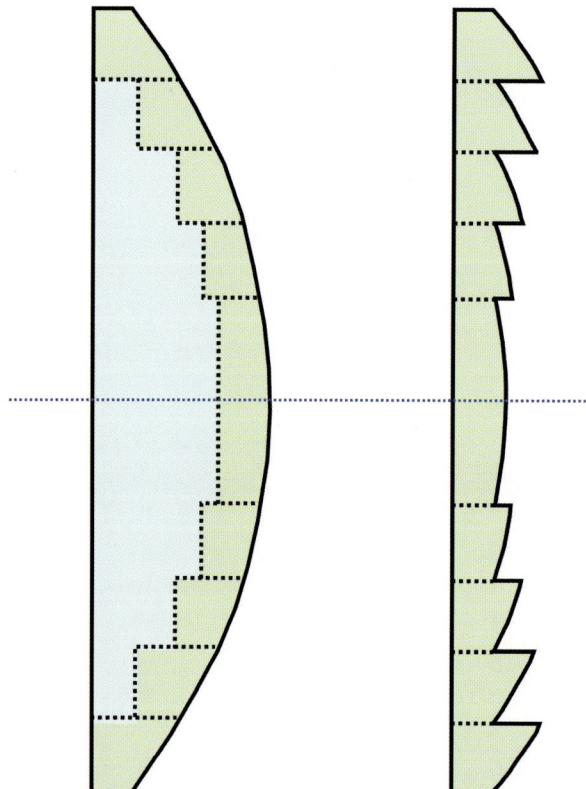

Cross-section of a convex lens and a Fresnel lens. (Wikimedia CC BY-SA 3.0/Philip Bosma)

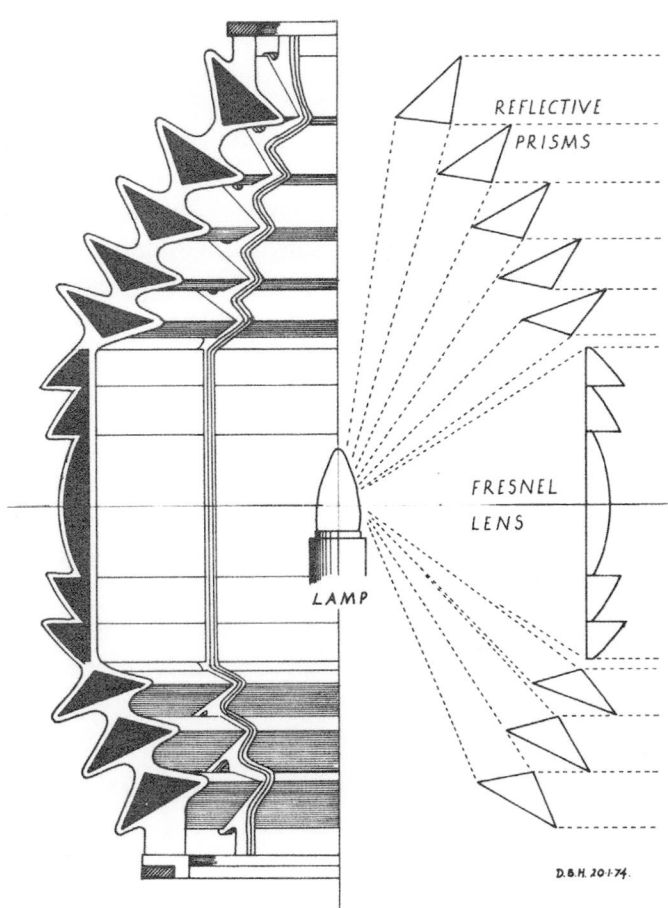

Diagram of a catadioptric Fresnel lens. (Douglas B. Hague)

lighthouses around the world. They vary in size and construction to meet the needs of the particular site. The size is classified into a number of orders, based on their focal length (distance between the light source and the lens). The largest commonly used ones are first order lenses, with a focal length of 920 mm, which are used for major landfall lights (although a few larger ones, called hyperradial lenses, have been built). These are around 2.5 m tall. They go down in size to sixth order lenses (focal length 150 mm, around 0.4–0.5 m tall), used on harbour piers and breakwaters. Some smaller seventh and eighth order ones are used in Scotland and Canada.

There are also two basic designs of Fresnel optics, the flashing or bull's-eye style and the fixed or beehive style. With flashing optics, the main lens is a circular bull's-eye design that focuses light into a beam. The optic will usually have several of these panels and will rotate to produce a flash of light every time one of the bull's eyes is pointing in the observer's direction; in between these times the light will not be visible.

The concept of a rotating flashing light was first introduced in 1757 by the Swede Jonas Norberg, who mounted several sets of lamps and reflectors on a base that was rotated using a clockwork mechanism. Prior to this all lighthouses showed a continuous light that was difficult to distinguish from other sources of light, including other lighthouses.

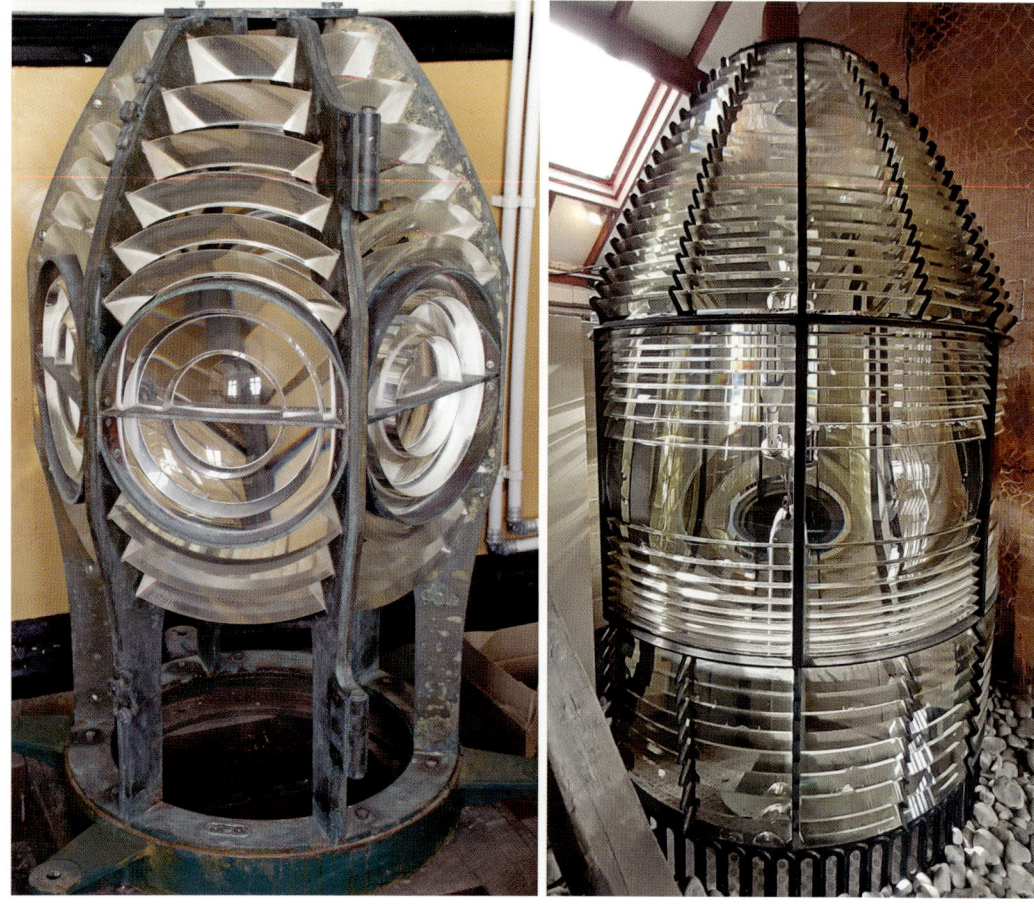

A fourth order flashing/bull's-eye optic at Skokholm lighthouse (left) and a first order fixed/ beehive optic from the Great Orme lighthouse (right), now on display at the Great Orme Visitor Centre.

The rotating system allowed each lighthouse to have its own character; for example, one could be set up to flash once every ten seconds, while another nearby one would flash twice, with a fifteen-second dark period between. The appendix to this book details the characters of all the Welsh lighthouses.

The clockwork mechanism that rotated the optic had weights on long cables that slowly dropped, causing the clockwork to operate. Many lighthouses will have a long metal tube running down the centre of the tower that accommodated the required cables. The keepers would need to regularly rewind the weights. Initially the optic would turn on wheels or a roller bearing system, but the friction of those with the heavy lenses would require very powerful mechanisms. Fresnel proposed turning the optics in a bath of mercury, a metal that is liquid at room temperature and is dense enough that the hundreds or thousands of pounds of metal and glass can float and rotate with minimal effort. It wasn't until 1890 that Leon Bourdelles developed a workable mercury system and it became widely used for larger optics.

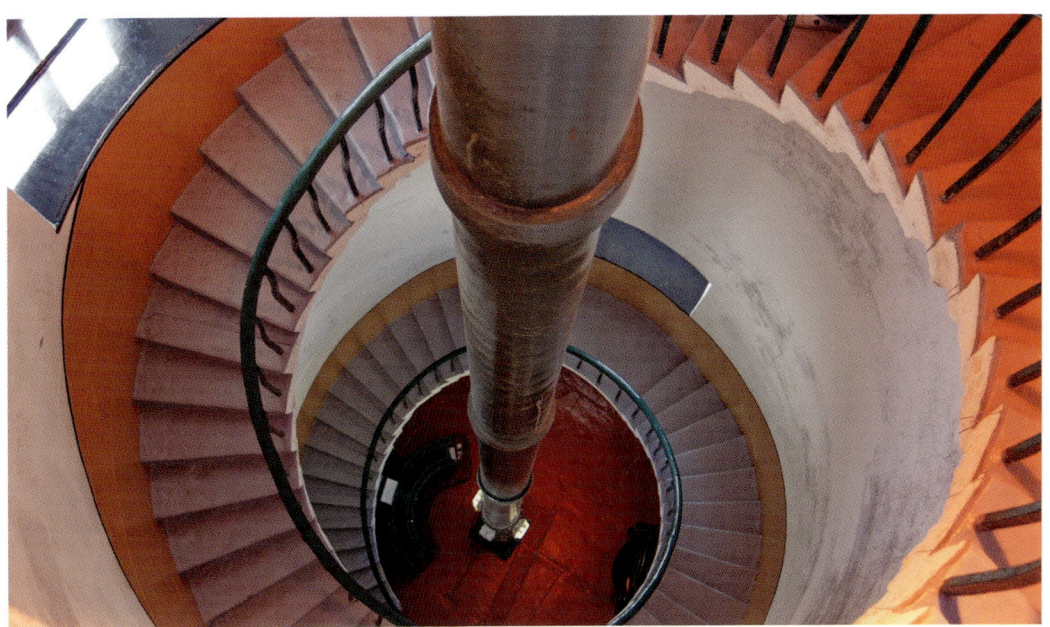

Circular staircase in the South Stack tower, with the tube containing the clockwork weights.

With the coming of electricity to lighthouses the clockwork was replaced with electric motors. And the development of flashing LED lamps means that rotating mechanisms are no longer necessary. The toxicity of the mercury means that these optics are now being removed for health and safety reasons. The ones at Skerries, Bardsey and Skokholm have already been decommissioned, and those at South Stack, Strumble Head, South Bishop and the Smalls will probably follow.

The second type of Fresnel lens, the fixed or beehive type, does not need to rotate. It is used either for a continuous light or with a lamp that can turn on and off to produce the flash itself, such as electric bulbs, or gas lamps equipped with a flashing mechanism like that invented by Dalén and described above. With these the central lens is toroidal, or a donut-shaped series of stepped lenses wrapped around the girth of the optic. Rather than producing beams of light, it will make a plane of light shining equally in all directions. Since these do not turn, they only need glass on the sides that actually shine out to sea, so will often have the back open, allowing easy access to the lamp within for maintenance. They are still in use at Point Lynas, St Ann's Head, Caldey and Flat Holm.

In Chapter 1 it was described how the two towers at St Ann's Head acted as leading lights, which guided mariners past dangerous rocks by lining up the lights. When one of the towers was decommissioned, that system was replaced by sector lighting. At St Ann's this utilises coloured filters mounted inside the lantern windows, so that the light passing through them appears red when the navigator is in an area of danger, near the offshore rocks. Similar filters can be seen at a number of other Welsh lighthouses, including Flat Holm, Caldey and Nash Point. In other Welsh lights, such as Porthcawl and Skokholm, separate highly directional lamps and lenses with different colours are used to shine out to the different sectors.

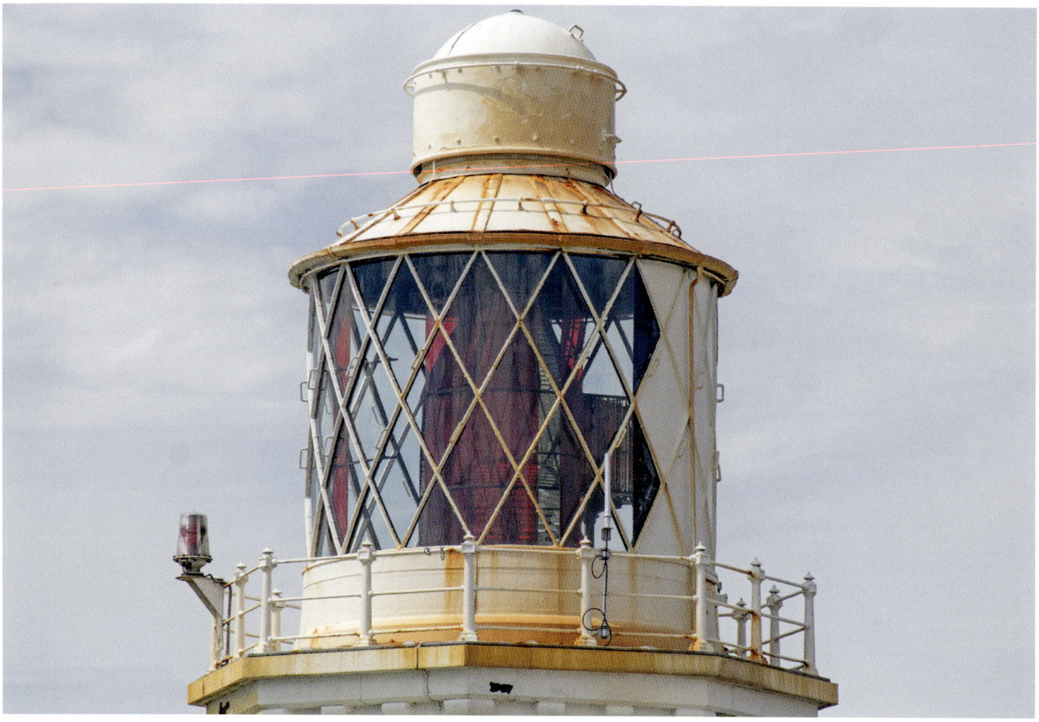

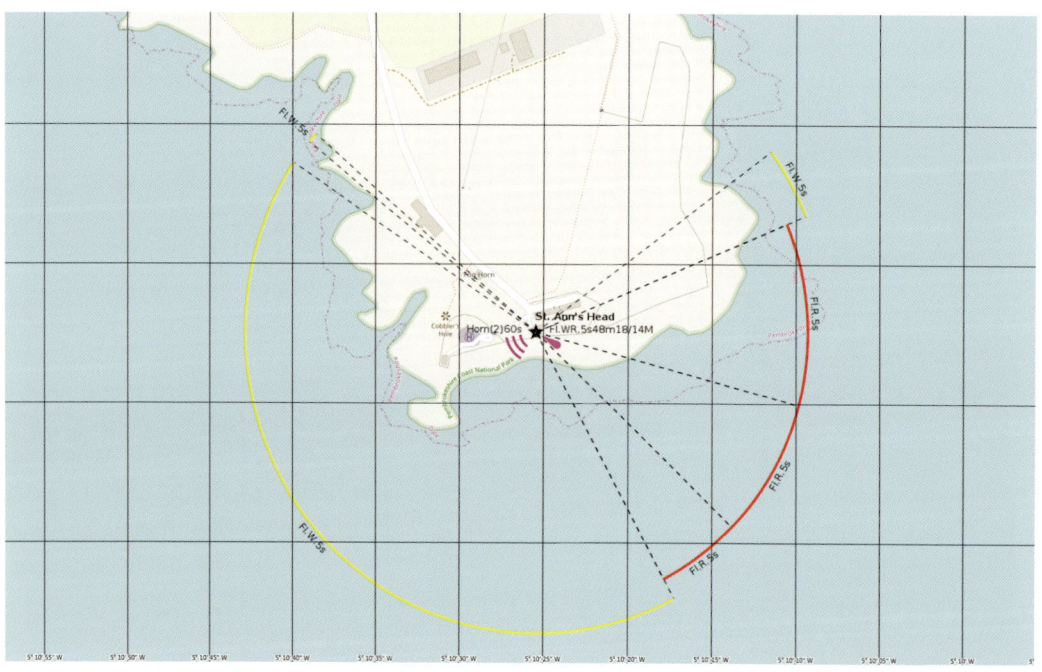

The lantern at St Ann's Head, showing the red sector filters.

Sea chart showing the character and red sector for St Ann's Head lighthouse. (Openseamap.org, CC BY-SA 2.0)

Fog Signals

So far in this book we've seen the improvement through the ages of lights that guide and alert mariners. However, sometimes the boundary between sea and sky disappears as fog descends, masking the lights no matter how powerful they are. In these conditions something else is needed to warn of nearby dangers.

Throughout the millennia sailors in foggy conditions relied on natural sounds to let them know they were near the coast, such as crashing waves or cliff-nesting seabirds. This was occasionally augmented by the sounding of trumpets, bells or explosives at fogbound lighthouses. It wasn't until the nineteenth century that new fog signals began to be developed.

South Stack is a good case study of the innovations and improvements in fog signals of all sorts. The lighthouse was first lit in 1809, but from around 1780 a bell had been rung in foggy conditions by the Holyhead harbour authorities on nearby North Stack, a clifftop overlooking the approach to the port. Soon after opening there were requests for a bell to be installed at the lighthouse, but that didn't happen until 1854. A massive 2-tonne bell, one of the largest bells anywhere in the UK, was then placed below the tower in an inverted position, with the opening pointing up. A clockwork mechanism caused a hammer to strike the bell slowly but continuously in foggy conditions. Although an impressive piece of equipment, there were many complaints that the bell couldn't always be heard clearly, particularly from upwind ships.

In 1857 Trinity House took over North Stack and installed two fog cannons. These guns would fire a charge every ten minutes, which could be heard from much further away than the bell. Attempts were made in 1869 to reposition the bell to improve its performance, but the guns were always superior. Guns continued to be used here until 1958, when an electrically powered signal was installed.

In 1895 the South Stack bell was replaced by a reed horn. This functions by forcing compressed air over a thin, flat reed (similar to one in a saxophone), producing a sound that is amplified by a large horn. A new building was constructed next to the tower to house the oil engine that compressed the air, and the two horns were mounted on the roof.

Around the turn of the twentieth century a new type of fog signal was developed in America that took advantage of the fact that sound travels further in water than in air. The submarine signal involved placing a sound emitter under water, as well as each ship having a hydrophone, a listening device mounted under the water line. In 1909 Trinity House trialled this system at South Stack, with a bell placed on the seabed between North and South Stack and an electrical cable running to an engine house. But regular faults developed in the striking mechanism. By 1925 it was decided to discontinue the system rather than pour more money into repairs.

In 1936, when the South Stack light was being electrified, a new diaphone foghorn system replaced the old reed horn. A diaphone works by having a slotted piston moving inside a similarly slotted cylinder. As compressed air is fed through the slots it makes a deep and far-carrying sound, ideal for a foghorn. At South Stack it was powered by a diesel generator and emitted the sound through two horns on the roof. It operated until 1964, when mains electricity arrived at the station. At that point an electric tannoy signal was installed. This used electric diaphragm sound emitters such as are used in speakers in a

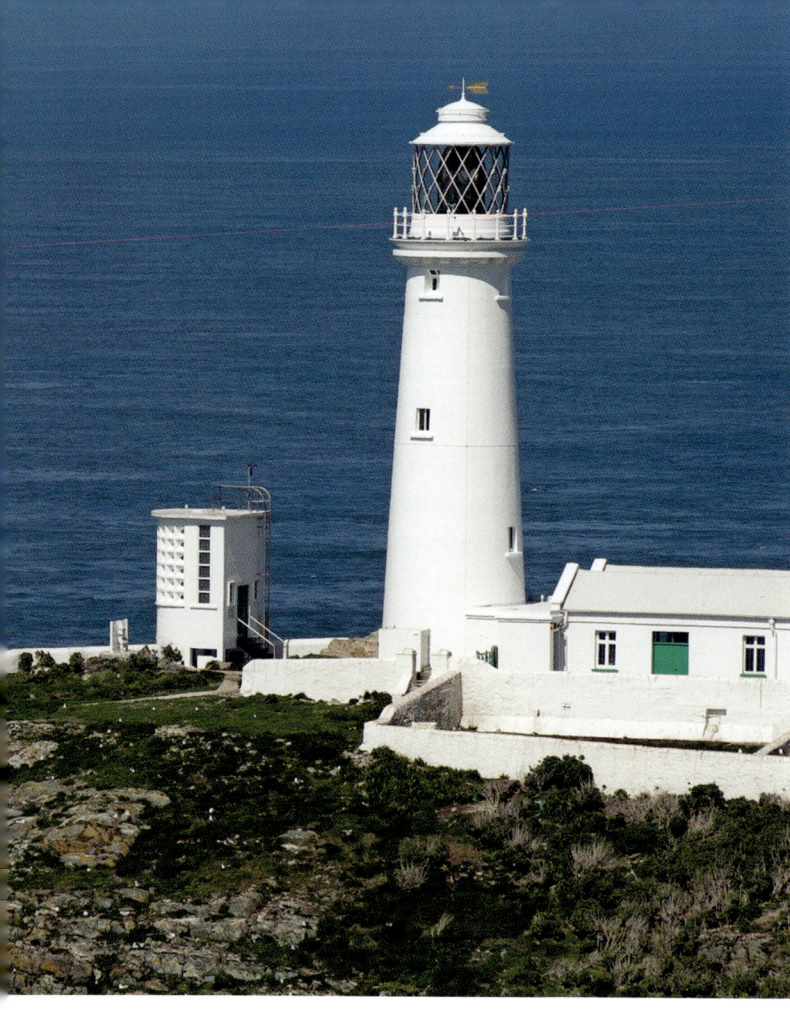

South Stack tower, with the electric tannoy foghorn to the left.

radio or TV. The sound from an individual horn is weaker, so these are deployed in large arrays of numerous speakers, like the sound system at a rock concert in a stadium.

South Stack was also the location of another unique innovation for use in foggy conditions. At 60 m above sea level, it has one of the highest lanterns in Wales. This means it can be obscured by particularly low cloud bases, even if visibility is better at sea and ship level. In 1831 Holyhead harbourmaster Captain Hugh Evans submitted a proposal to Trinity House to build a moveable low light for use in the fog. This consisted of a rail track on a steep incline leading down to the water level. A cabin on wheels, with windows facing out to sea, would contain a set of lamps that could be lit and lowered down to sea level during foggy conditions, shining out underneath the fog. A light this low would not carry as far past the sea level horizon as the tower light would, but in the circumstances would be better than nothing. The system was built in just a few months and continued in use until 1880. At that point a new permanent low light was built on the western tip of the island, with steps leading down to it protected by walls. The installation of a much brighter lamp in the tower in 1906 meant the low light was rarely used, so was removed.

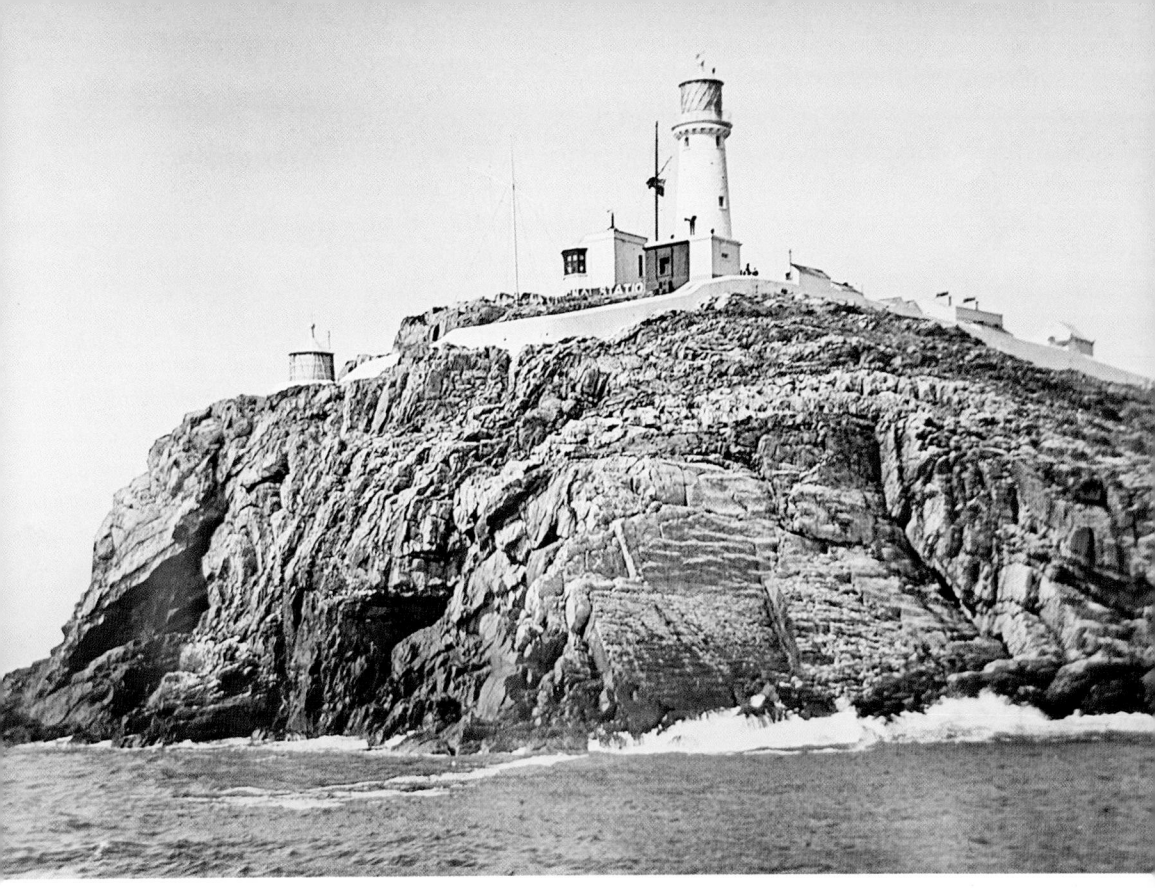

South Stack from the sea, *c.* 1900. The low light lantern can be seen on the left. The foghorn building is in front of the tower.

A little under half of the lighthouses in Wales are known to have had fog signals. Bells were used at the Smalls, South Bishop, the Holyhead and Fishguard breakwaters, and Trwyn Du, but they were all much smaller than the South Stack one. The first three were replaced by horns many years ago. In 2020 Trinity House announced they would disable the bell at Trwyn Du, which had rung every thirty seconds around the clock for a hundred years, and replace it with an electrical signal. This caused great consternation locally from those who loved its evocative sound, but the plans went ahead despite petitions and it was silenced in 2022.

When horns of various types were installed, they were usually housed in buildings next to the towers that contained engines to compress air, although at Skokholm they were in the main lighthouse building. Mindful of the loud and persistent sound that the larger horns would produce, sites with ample space (Flat Holm, Nash Point, St Ann's Head) had the foghorns in separate buildings a good distance from the keepers' accommodation.

Conversion to electricity led to multi-speaker tannoy arrays to be installed not only at South Stack, but also at North Stack, Bardsey, Strumble Head and St Ann's Head. Modern developments have brought in much more compact devices, which can easily be mounted on a ledge, such as the Essi FW/6 signal at Mumbles lighthouse.

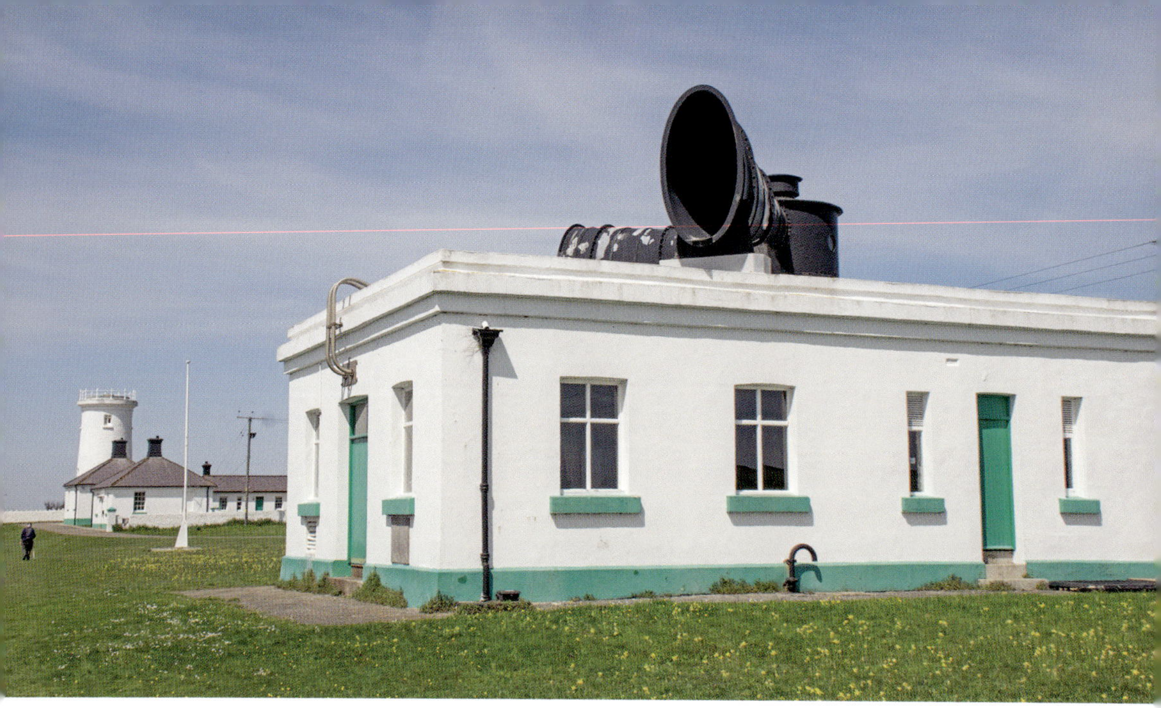

Foghorn building at Nash Point.

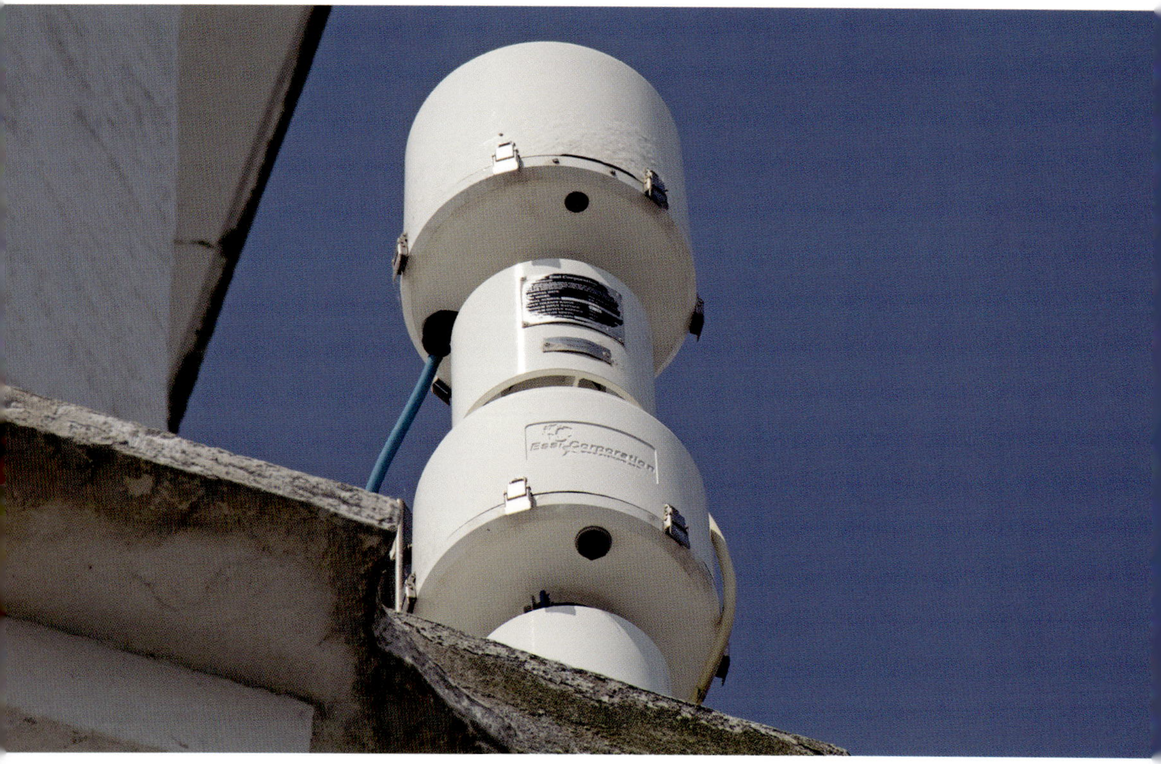

Electronic fog signal at Mumbles.

CHAPTER 4

People

The Builders

Lighthouses are specialist structures that often require novel building techniques. In particular, those exposed to the forces of the sea need the strength and resistance to remain standing, fulfilling their purpose of shining a light. Britain and Ireland boasted several dedicated lighthouse designers and builders, often with sons and grandsons following in their footsteps. In other cases, established engineers for major harbour authorities, such as Liverpool, also designed the lighthouses that guided the way to their ports.

Henry Whiteside

The earliest known, and most unusual, lighthouse builder in Wales was Henry Whiteside. He is renowned as the builder of the first lighthouse on the Smalls Rock, 29 km off the coast of Pembrokeshire, a feat described in Chapter 1. He was born around 1746 in Liverpool and was apprenticed as a carpenter in 1764. He went on to build musical instruments, but in 1774 he made an unlikely change of profession when he submitted a design for the Smalls lighthouse. It was accepted and he led the team building the lighthouse, finishing in 1776.

He stayed on at the lighthouse with the keepers to observe how well it worked, but they were marooned in severe winter storms. Running short of water and fuel for the lamp, in desperation they wrote letters pleading for their rescue, which they then launched in wooden casks to float to shore. One arrived in just a few days and they were soon rescued.

After his lighthouse work was complete Whiteside settled in Solva, his base when constructing the lighthouse. In 1780 he married Martha Bevan, daughter of the keeper of the inn where Whiteside had first lodged. He built a house on the field where he had originally assembled the lighthouse structure; they lived there until his death in 1824. In his will he left several houses in his native Liverpool as well as properties in Solva to his wife and his sister Anne. Martha and Henry are buried in Whitchurch churchyard near Solva.

William Jernegan

Two early lighthouses in Swansea were built by a man with a more traditional architectural background. William Jernegan was the son of a carpenter, Thomas, and was baptised in St Peter le Poer parish in the City of London on 6 May 1753. At the age of fourteen he was apprenticed to another carpenter and builder, Luffman Atterbury (who was also a well-known singer, composer and harpsichordist in his spare time) until 1770, when he returned to work with his father.

He appears to have wound up in Swansea in the mid-1770s as an assistant to English architect John Johnson, who was building two fine houses there. He stayed on and developed his own architectural practice, designing a large number of mansions and Regency terraces, as well as the Swansea Assembly Rooms and several churches and chapels. He also erected some buildings in Milford Haven, including the Customs House (now a museum).

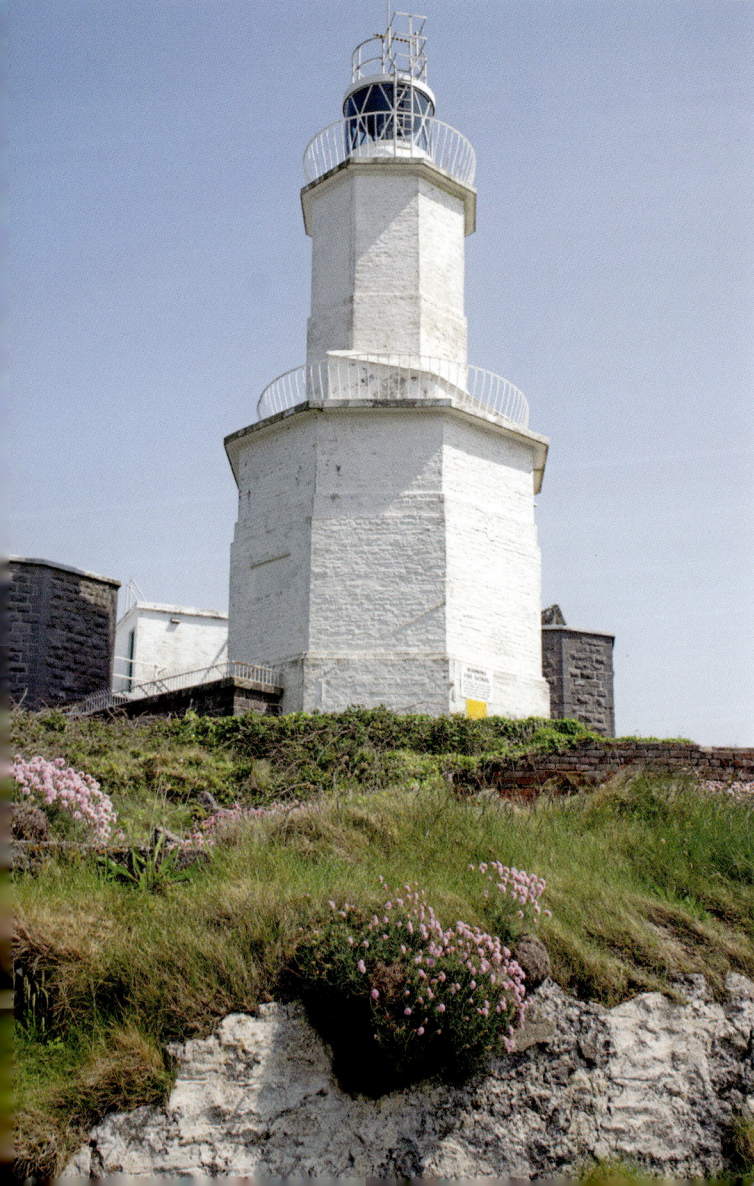

Mumbles lighthouse.

Following the collapse during construction of the Mumbles lighthouse in 1792 Jernegan was called in to come up with a new and elegant octagonal design, which was completed in 1794. When the Swansea West Pier was extended in 1803 he was asked to plan a new lighthouse, also octagonal but this time made of cast iron.

He died at his home in Adelaide Place in Swansea in 1836. He never married, so he left his entire estate to his friend James Hall, the town surveyor for Swansea (except for £100 and his bed bequeathed to his servant, Mary Ann Sears).

Daniel Asher Alexander

When permission was given in 1808 to build South Stack lighthouse, Trinity House tasked their newly appointed Consultant Engineer Daniel Alexander with producing a design. Alexander was born in 1768 in Southwark, London, son of felt-maker Daniel Alexander and his wife, Elizabeth Humphreys. He was educated at St Paul's school, then entered the Royal Academy School at the age of fourteen, where he won a silver medal for architecture.

In 1796 he was appointed Surveyor for the London Dock Company, a position he held until 1820, responsible for designing all new buildings in the docks. He also drew up plans for prisons at Dartmoor and Maidstone. From 1807 he acted as a consultant for Trinity House. After designing South Stack, he went on to build several more lighthouses, including ones at Harwich, Lundy Island, Inner Farne, Heligoland and Hurst.

In 1792 Alexander married Catherine Pattenden, but she died in 1798, three years after the birth of their only son, Daniel. Two years later he married Anna Maria Broadley, with whom he had eight more children. The family moved to Blackheath, Kent, then to Yarmouth, Isle of Wight. He retired to Exeter, where he died in 1846. He was interred back in Yarmouth, where a plaque in St James' Church commemorates him and his wife.

Joseph Nelson

Although Daniel Alexander designed South Stack lighthouse, the man responsible for the day-to-day operation of constructing it was Joseph Nelson. He was born in 1777 in Batley, West Yorkshire, into a stonemason family. His father, William, was a mason as was his grandfather John Nelson (who was also a well-known Methodist preacher).

Nelson had been working as a foreman at the London Docks when Alexander chose him to supervise the building of South Stack. The two later worked together to erect lighthouses at Inner Farne and Longstone Rock, as well as Lundy. Nelson also built an unusual octagonal wooden lighthouse tower, emerging from the top of the keeper's cottage, on Braunton Sands in Devon. He went back to Wales in 1821 to construct the square tower on Bardsey, then to Caldey Island in 1829 to build the lighthouse there. His last work in Wales was the two lights at Nash Point in 1832.

He then returned to Yorkshire, where he settled briefly in Newsam Green and died in March 1833 at the age of fifty-five. He never married but his will left all his estate to his siblings and their families. His gravestone in St Peter's Church, Birstall, where he was baptised, sings his praises as a lighthouse engineer.

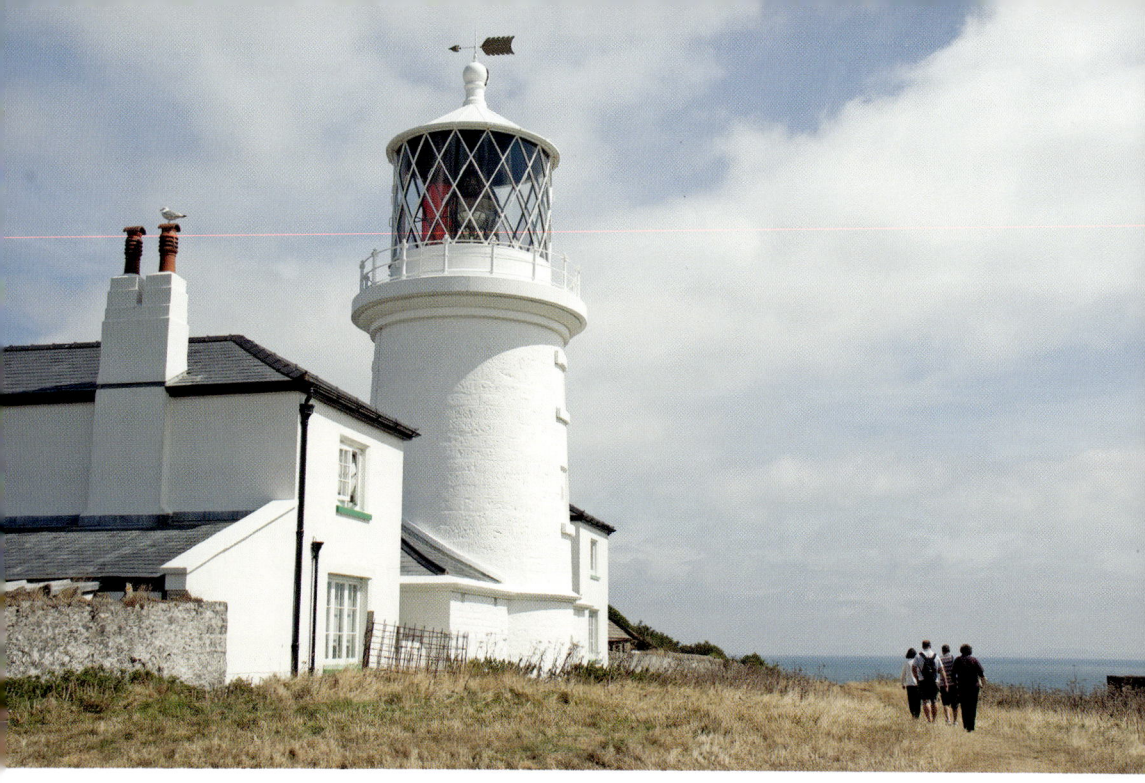

Caldey Island lighthouse.

James Walker

One of the titans of British lighthouse building, and civil engineering in general, was James Walker. He was born in Falkirk, Scotland, in 1781 to merchant James Walker and Margaret Smith. After being educated at Glasgow University, he began work in 1800 in London with his uncle Ralph Walker, who was an engineer developing the West India Docks. He rapidly became a very productive and well-regarded engineer, eventually being appointed the second president of the Institution of Civil Engineers after the death of the first, Thomas Telford, in 1834.

Walker became the consultant engineer for Trinity House and designed his first lighthouse, West Usk, in 1820. He eventually built more than twenty lighthouses for Trinity House, including several in Wales: Nash Point (1832, in conjunction with Joseph Nelson), Trwyn Du (1838), South Bishop (1839), the now-removed piled lighthouse offshore at Point of Ayr (1844), Skerries (1848) and his finest and most challenging one, the rock tower on the Smalls (1861). He focused on not only building sturdy and useful towers, but also attractive accommodation and suitable sanitation provision.

In 1813 he married his childhood friend Janet Cook in Falkirk. They had two daughters, but Janet sadly died in 1823. He died in 1862 at his home in Great George Street, Westminster, just across the street from the grand headquarters of his beloved Institution of Civil Engineers. He was buried in St John Episcopal Graveyard, Edinburgh, Scotland, alongside his daughter Margaret, who had been living there and died young, and his wife.

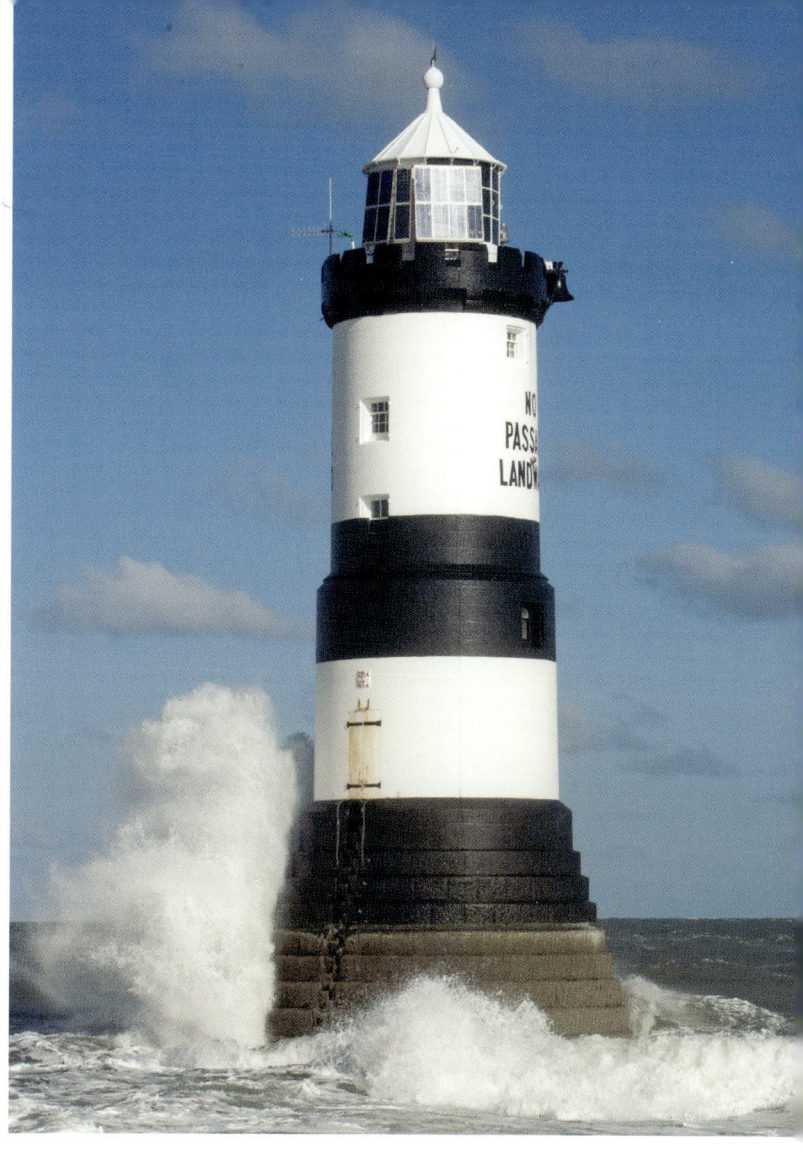

Trwyn Du lighthouse,
Penmon, Anglesey.

John Rennie

Another well-known civil engineer who was involved with lighthouses was John Rennie. He was born in 1761 to James and Jean Rennie, farmers in Phantassie, Haddingtonshire (now East Lothian). His interest in machinery was encouraged by local millwright Andrew Meikle, leading to Rennie eventually setting up his own millwright business. He was introduced to James Watt, who invited him to become involved in using his newly invented steam engine for milling. In 1790 his business interests expanded and he began surveying for the construction of the Kennet & Avon Canal. This led to his distinguished career in building both canals and harbours.

Lighthouses were a minor part of his output. He was involved in building the famous Bell Rock lighthouse near Arbroath, although there has been controversy over who should take greater credit, Rennie or the original designer, Robert Stevenson. In Wales he was behind the major redevelopment of Holyhead Harbour. He first started drawing up the plans in 1809, and construction continued on into 1821. He also improved the harbour at Howth, near Dublin, Ireland, at the other end of the Holyhead–Dublin packet ship route. At both places he designed identical and elegant lighthouses on the piers. Both still stand today, with few modifications.

Rennie died in 1821 before the Holyhead works were finished. He and his wife Martha Ann Mackintosh had nine children, two of whom also went on to be distinguished engineers. Rennie was buried in St Paul's Cathedral in London.

Jesse Hartley

Many ships sail around the coast of North Wales on the approach to the great port of Liverpool. So, it is not surprising that the harbour authorities were involved in setting up lighthouses along the coast to the west. One of their main architects was Jesse Hartley. He was born in 1780 in Pontefract, Yorkshire, son of a builder and architect. His father, Bernard, involved him in bridge-building projects from an early age. He struck out on his

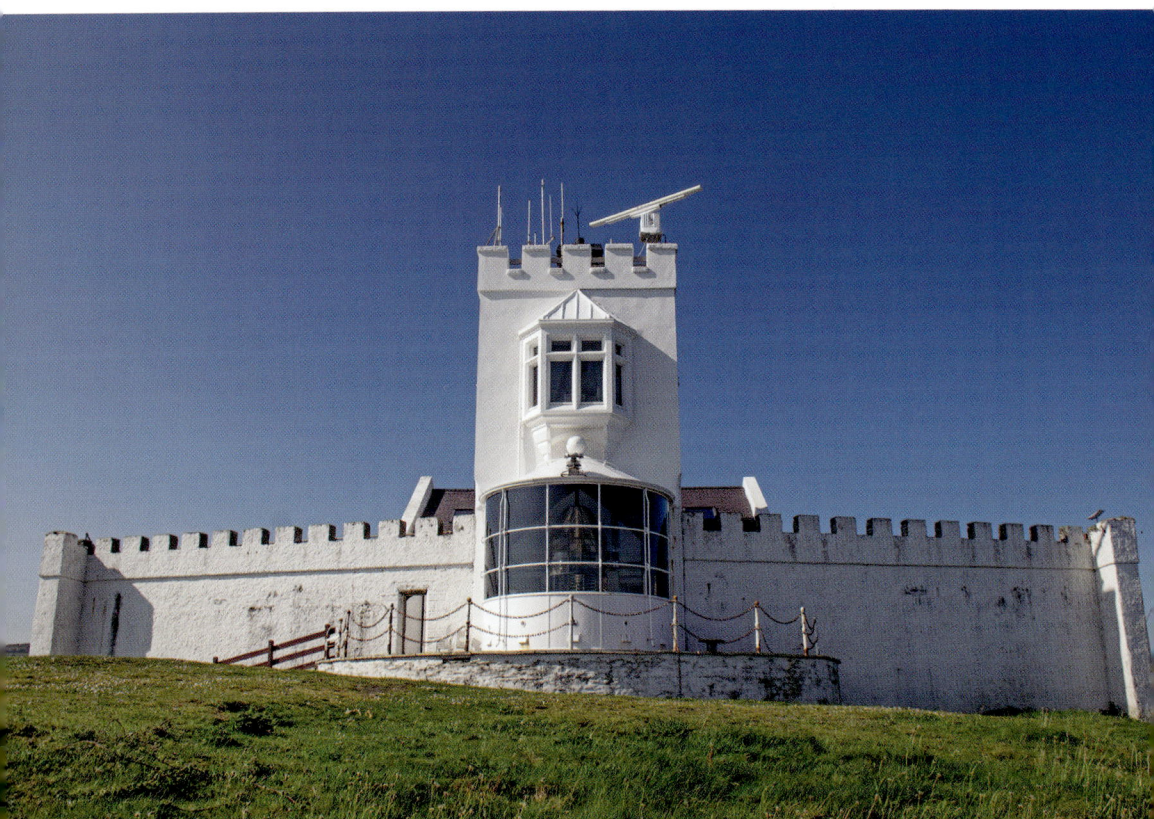

Point Lynas lighthouse, Anglesey.

own to design and maintain bridges in Salford and Dungarvan, Ireland (where he met his wife, Ellenor Penney).

In 1824 he was hired as the head surveyor by the Liverpool Dock trustees. His best-known work there was the designing of the Albert Docks. But he was also called on to improve the light at Point Lynas, Anglesey, where pilots joined ships to guide them to Liverpool. Sited atop cliffs at the end of the peninsula, the upside-down lighthouse, with the lantern at ground level and observation rooms above, was built in a delightful castellated style. It was first lit in 1835.

Hartley remained as port surveyor for thirty-six years. He is reputed to have been in the office up to three days before his death in 1860 at the age of seventy-nine. His only son, John Bernard Hartley, was appointed his successor but had to retire early due to ill health. Jesse and his wife are buried at St Mary's Church, Bootle.

George Fosbery Lyster

The successor to the Hartleys at Liverpool Docks was George Fosbery Lyster. He was born in 1821 in Mount Talbot, Co. Roscommon, Ireland, into a landed family with Yorkshire roots. After being educated at King William's College, Isle of Man, he trained as a civil engineer under James Meadows Rendel (another president of the Institution of Civil Engineers). He then worked on dock facilities on the River Shannon in Limerick, moved to Holyhead as the assistant resident engineer at the harbour, then went to Guernsey harbour as engineer-in-chief. In 1861 he was appointed engineer-in-chief for Liverpool Harbour, a position he held for most of the rest of his life.

Lyster's work at Liverpool greatly improved the docks, particularly across the river at Birkenhead, which the Liverpool authority had taken over in 1858. His main lighthouse work began soon after he took up the job. It was decided that a new light was needed along the North Wales coast approaching Liverpool and Lyster chose a site on the Great Orme, near Llandudno, and drew up the plans. It was completed in just a year and was first lit on 1 December 1862. In the 1870s Lyster was also involved in planning additions to the Point Lynas lighthouse, including building extensions that reflected the original castellated design.

While in Holyhead Lyster married Martha Sanderson, daughter of Thomas Sanderson, speaker of the colonial assembly on the Caribbean island of Antigua. They had four children. As Lyster went into semi-retirement in the 1890s, he spent more time at his country residence Plas Isaaf, Ruthin, Denbighshire. In 1897 his son Anthony formally succeeded him as chief engineer, and George died in 1899.

Sir James Nicholas Douglass

Another lighthouse-building dynasty was the Douglass family. Nicholas Douglass, who was born in Ryton near Newcastle upon Tyne, began working for Trinity House in 1839, rising to become the superintendent engineer. His two sons, James (b. 1826) and William (b. 1831), followed in his footsteps, as did James' son William Tregarthen Douglass.

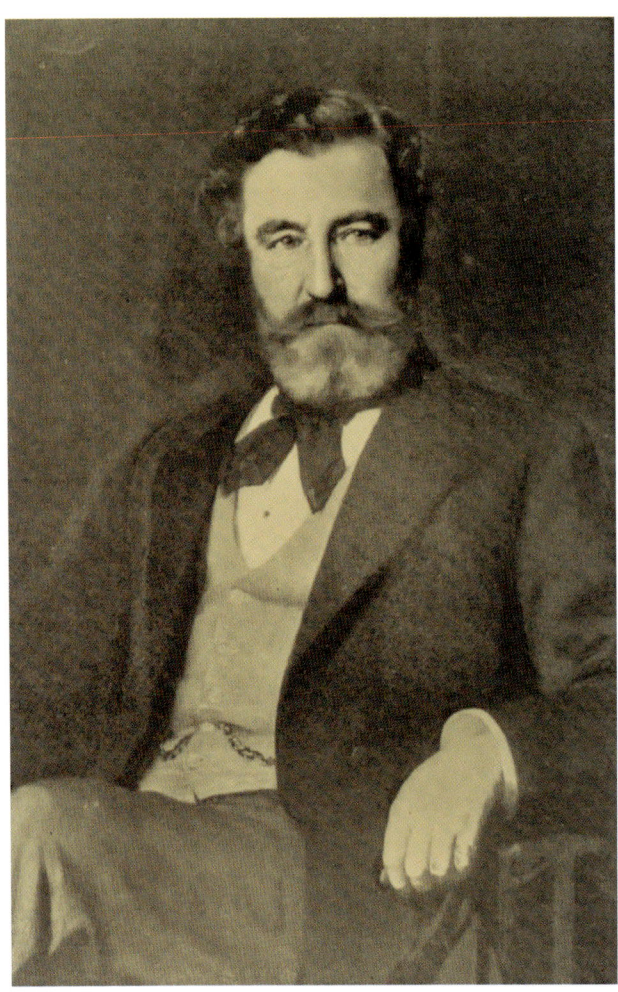

James Douglass.

James was born in Bromley-by-Bow, East London, and by 1841 the family were living in Tenby. They moved to the Isles of Scilly, where James assisted his father in building the Bishop Rock lighthouse. He went on to build piled lighthouses in the Thames Estuary, then returned to Wales to become resident engineer for building the Smalls lighthouse, from 1855 to 1861. Shortly after he succeeded James Walker as the Engineer-in-Chief at Trinity House. He went on to build twenty lighthouses for the organisation, including Great Castle Head in Milford Haven (1870) and on St Tudwal's island off the Llŷn peninsula (1877). He was also involved in many projects to improve lighting systems, including experimenting with Argand and electric arc lamps with John Tyndall and Michael Faraday.

Douglass was knighted in 1882 after the completion of his most famous work, the current Eddystone lighthouse. He was also on the council of the Institution of Civil Engineers and a Fellow of the Royal Society. In 1854 he married Mary Tregarthen, daughter of a ship owner in the Isles of Scilly, and had eight children. He retired to Bonchurch, Isle of Wight, in 1894, where he died in 1898.

Sir Thomas Matthews

James Douglass' successor as Engineer-in-Chief for Trinity House was Thomas Matthews. He was born in 1849 in Madron, Penzance, Cornwall, son of the borough surveyor John Matthews. He assisted his father in developing the harbour and sea defences, as well as providing drinking water for the town, then in 1874 he joined Trinity House as an assistant engineer, working under James Douglass.

He became chief construction assistant engineer in 1879, rising to Engineer-in-Chief on Douglass' retirement. During his tenure his Welsh works included designing the Skokholm lighthouse, finished in 1916, and overseeing alterations at Nash Point and Bardsey and the building of Strumble Head and East Usk. He also further developed light-buoys, beacons and lighthouse oil burners.

In 1875 he married Mary Annie Frances Blackwell, daughter of an innkeeper in his birth village of Madron, and they had six children. Matthews was knighted in 1909 and retired from Trinity House in 1915. He settled in Torquay, Devon, where he died in 1930.

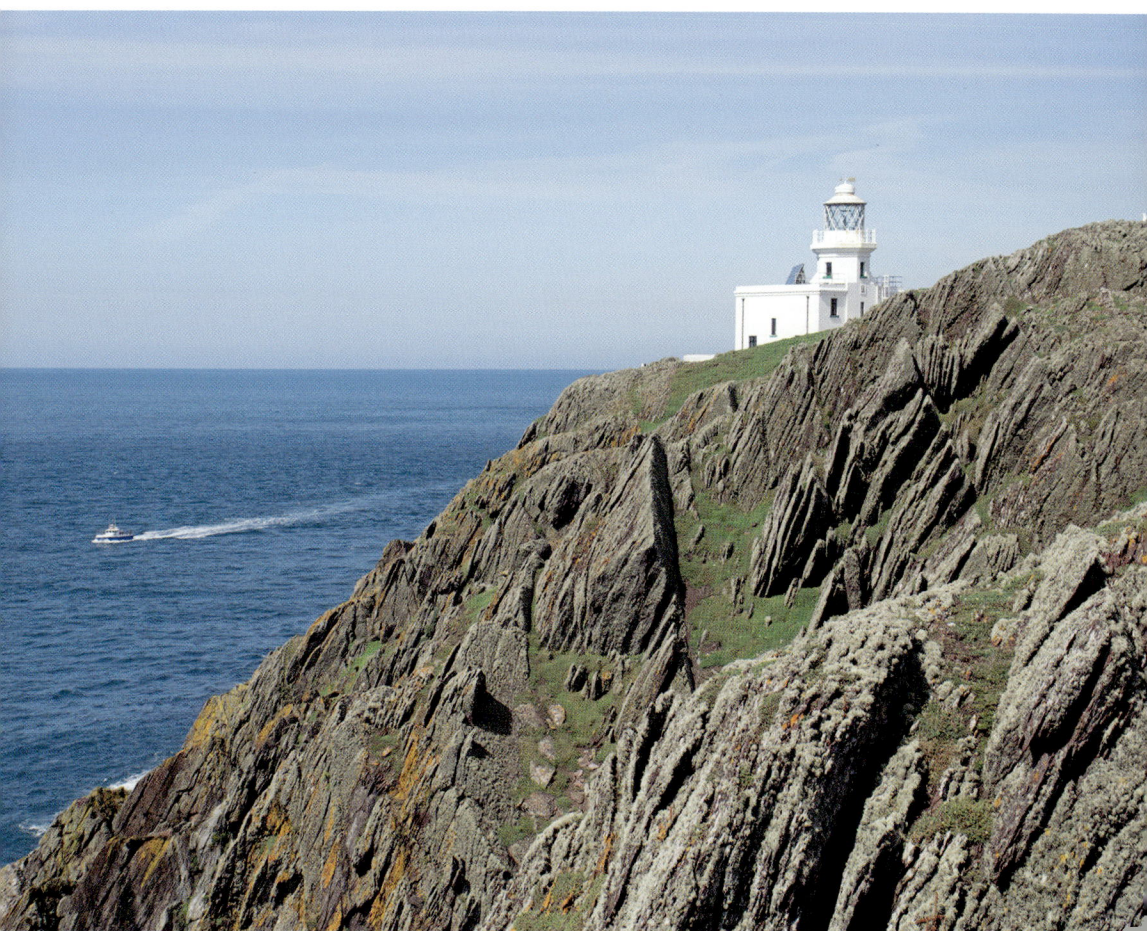

Skokholm lighthouse.

The Keepers and Their Families

Two recent films, both confusingly titled *The Lighthouse*, paint a dark and broody picture of the lives of lighthouse keepers. The 2016 movie, starring Mark Lewis Jones and Michael Jibson, is based on a true story from Wales at the Smalls lighthouse, whereas the 2019 one, with Robert Pattinson and Willem Dafoe, is set in New England. Both in the psychological thriller/horror genre, they of course don't reflect the true nature of the everyday life of the keepers and their families. Let's explore the real lives of lighthouse keepers.

The primary role of a lighthouse keeper is to keep the light shining. Any failure of the beacon that mariners rely on to guide them on their way could result in tragedy. So, someone had to be keeping watch at all times, night and day. Most lighthouses would be manned with three keepers: a principal keeper (PK), who was in charge, and two assistant keepers (AK). They would work in a rota, with one person on duty at all times. The shifts would alternate so the same person wasn't always on at night. A typical rota would be for a keeper to work 4 a.m. to midday and 8 p.m. to midnight on the first day, then midday to 8 p.m. on the second day, and midnight to 4 a.m. on the third day, with the rest of that day off.

And there was a lot to do when on watch, particularly in the days before electrification. Oil and paraffin lamps' wicks needed to be trimmed regularly and the fuel needed to

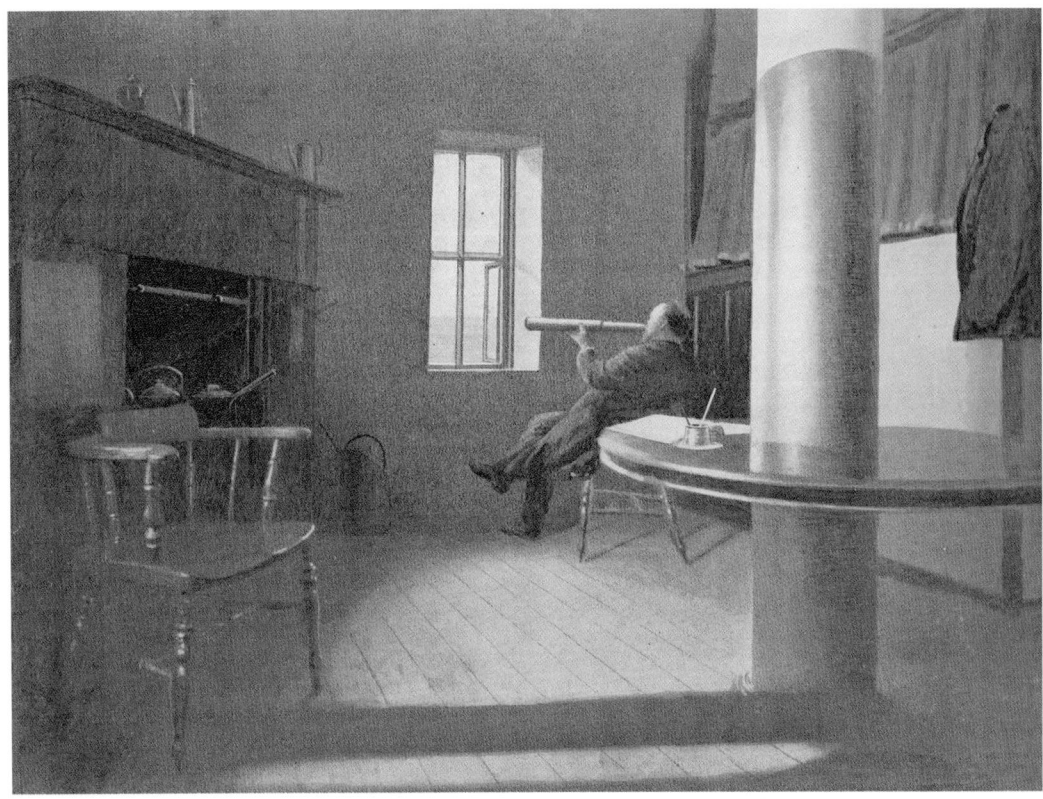

The lighthouse keeper on watch at Holyhead Breakwater, *c.* 1897.

be checked and replenished often. They had to be lit at dusk and extinguished at dawn. Rotating optics were run by clockwork mechanisms that needed to be wound several times a day. Other duties included recording weather data throughout the day and monitoring passing ships. Regular tests of radio contact with other nearby lighthouses and coast guard stations were carried out.

Even when not officially on watch there were lots of tasks to undertake. Cleanliness was paramount and lenses, reflectors and lantern windows had to be cleaned regularly. The working and living spaces needed to be kept tidy and dust free and the brass hand rails and other fittings were polished to a bright shine. Electrical generators and other equipment were well maintained and kept running smoothly. Larger projects, like painting the tower and outbuildings or repairing roads to the jetty, were also the responsibility of the keepers. Trinity House made regular surprise inspections, so there was no slacking.

Keepers at shore stations, where the lighthouse is easily accessible by road, lived with their families in the usual domestic situations. But at offshore lighthouses on islands or rocks the keepers were the only ones there, so needed to take care of all day-to-day tasks themselves. This included the cooking. Feeding themselves was an integral part of the rota and they would take turns preparing the meals for the whole crew. A large midday meal

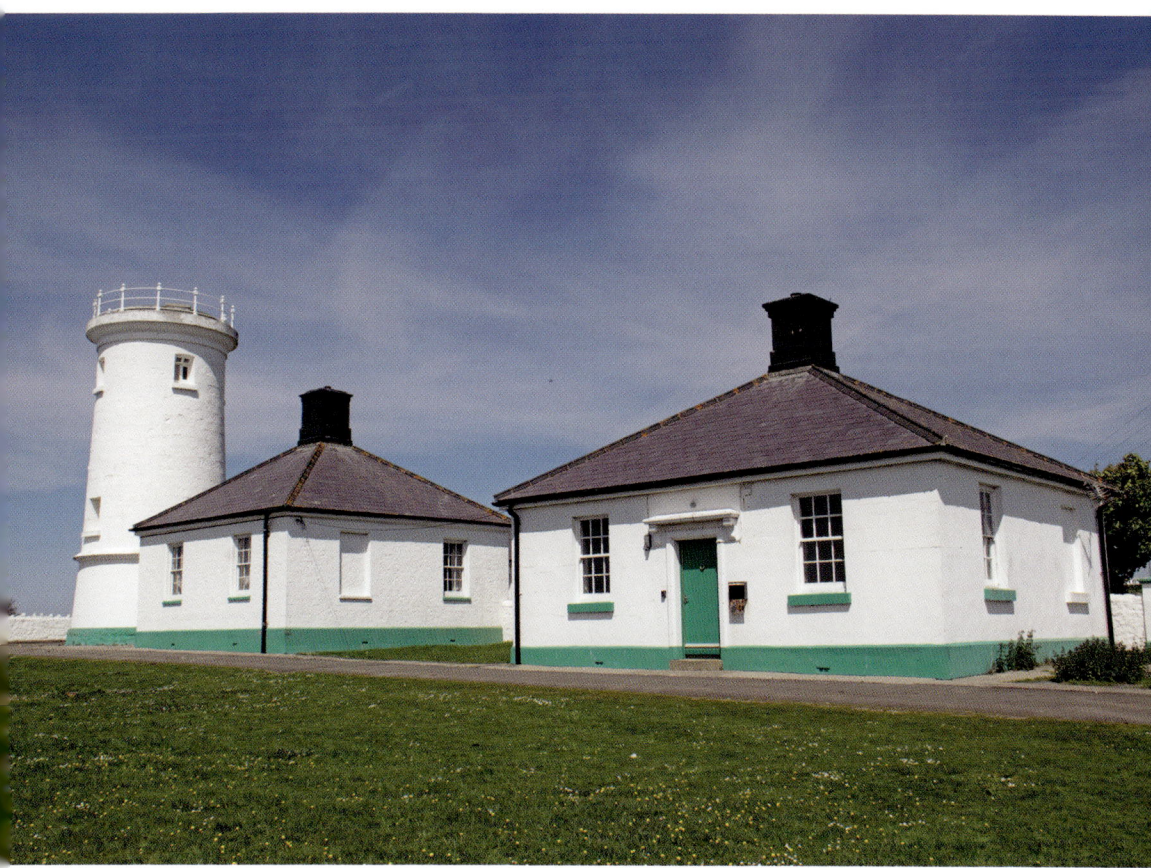

Freshly painted keepers' cottages at Nash Point lower lighthouse.

was the time for everyone to get together, prepared by the off-duty keeper who ruled the kitchen that day. Part of the training given to new recruits by Trinity House was in cooking, particularly baking bread.

On offshore stations the keepers would spend a month on shore leave at home with their families. On return they had to bring back all the provisions they would need for the next several weeks. Fresh meat and vegetables were highly prized, but in the days before freezers they would only last the first few days. After that they would have to rely on tinned meat, fruit and vegetables until the next keeper came back from shore leave. At stations where there was enough room the keepers would have gardens, usually in walled enclosures to protect them from the elements. Digging and weeding were part of their regular duties.

Despite the large number of tasks that the keepers had to attend to, there was still plenty of time to fill. The pace of life was unhurried, and most jobs were done slowly and meticulously. Even then, there was time for other pursuits. Building model ships in bottles is the classic maritime hobby taken up by many keepers. Other types of crafts, such as woodcarving, painting or knitting, would also be pursued. Fishing was popular and fulfilled a dual role of also keeping fresh food on the table.

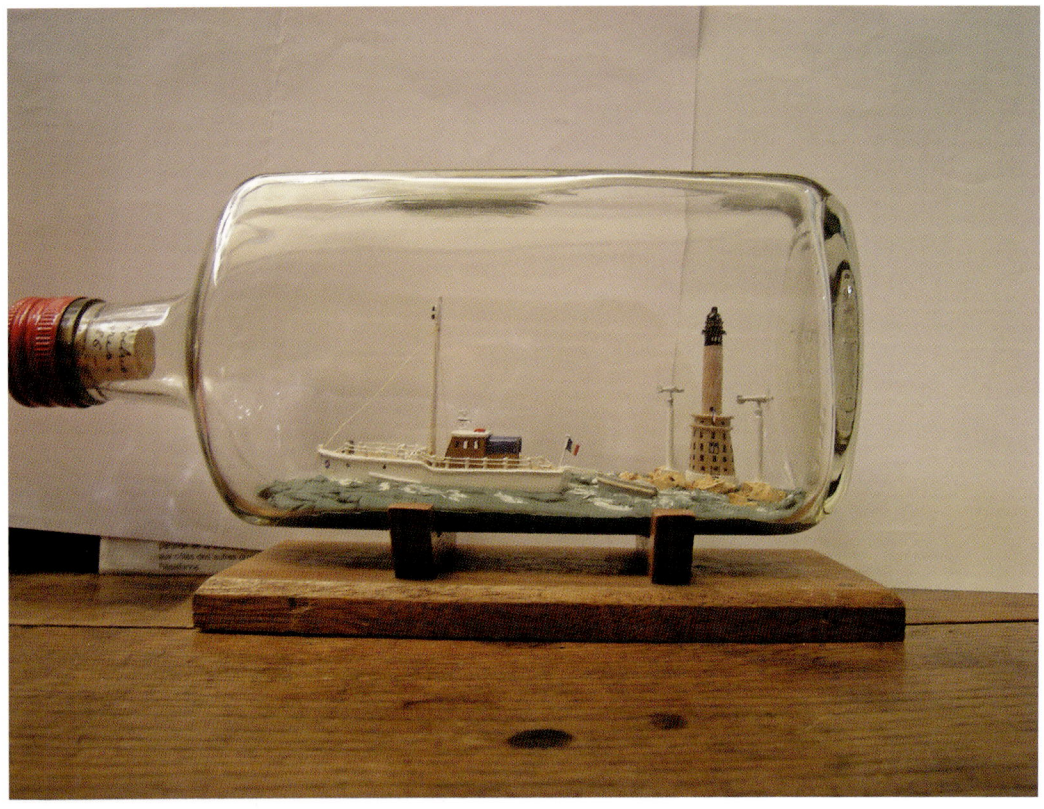

Models of the ship *La Horaine* and the lighthouse at Roches-Douvres, France, in a bottle, made by keeper François Jouas-Poutrel in the late twentieth century. (Wikimedia CC BY-SA 3.0/ Barbetorte)

Lighthouses were usually in areas with rich fauna and flora and many keepers took a keen interest in the plants, birds and other wildlife around their station. Reading was also a popular pastime and there would be plenty of books around. On offshore stations the relief boats would often bring along a pile of the recent newspapers that would keep the keepers occupied for days with reading and discussions. Those with a more literary bent would do their own writing: poetry, fiction or journals. Boardgames such as chess or Scrabble were also popular. When televisions started appearing at lighthouses alongside electrification they eventually filled many of the gaps in off-duty time.

Station Stories

The idyllic picture below of West Usk lighthouse shows the keeper and his family. The youngest son proudly shows off his bicycle, while his older brothers perch on the wall (which they had probably helped to whitewash), and the youngest, the only daughter, stays close to her mother. This is James William Parsons and his family. The family moved here in 1894 after spending seven years at Orfordness lighthouse in Suffolk.

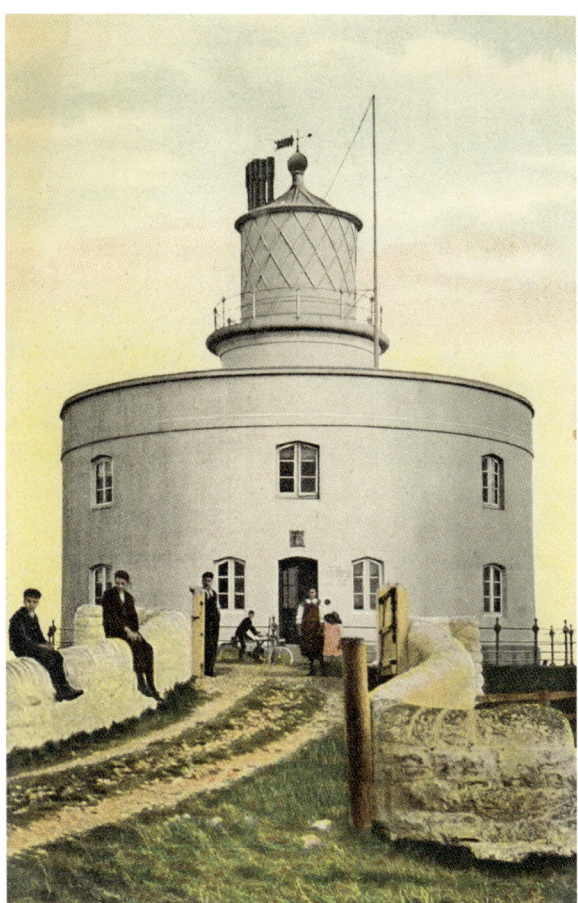

The Parsons family at West Usk lighthouse, c. 1902. Left to right: Henry Bowen, William James, keeper James William, Arthur Felton, Mary Jane and Dorothy Helena Parsons.

Both James and his wife, Mary Jane, grew up in lighthouses. James' father (also James) was previously a butler in London but joined the lighthouse service in 1862 when his son was just two years old. His first posting was Les Hanois in Guernsey, but in 1865 he became Assistant Keeper at Trwyn Du (then called Menai lighthouse), on Anglesey. The Principal Keeper there was Henry Bowen. He had previously been keeper at South Stack and was responsible for installing the giant fog bell. Among his nine children was Mary Jane, who was born at South Stack. Mary Jane was just two years younger than James and the two grew up together living in adjacent keepers' cottages. They went their own ways, James becoming a keeper in 1879, starting at Lundy Island, and Mary Jane moving to Criccieth with her mother after her father's death and becoming a dressmaker. However, the two kept in touch, and in 1888 they were married.

The lighthouse at West Usk and its nearby beach was a popular tourist destination for day-trippers from Newport, and James and his family would take visitors to the top of the lighthouse. One day in 1900 a day-tripper went into the sea for a swim and never returned. His body was later found by one of James' sons.

None of the Parsons' children followed them into the lighthouse life. The eldest, William James, became a carpenter in Cardiff. Henry Bowen did teacher training at St Luke's College in Exeter and became a schoolmaster in suburban North London. Arthur Felton became a grocer's assistant and later travelling salesman, based in Weston-super-Mare. Sadly, little Dorothy Helena died shortly after this photograph was taken. After all the children had left home James and Mary continued working lighthouses together, at Caldey Island in 1911 and Burnham lighthouse in Somerset in 1921, where she was officially listed as the Assistant Keeper.

At most lighthouses in Wales keepers would be moved around to different stations every few years, as they progressed through their careers from Assistant to Principal Keeper. However, Mumbles lighthouse was run by the Swansea Harbour Trust, and things were done differently than at Trinity House (who eventually took over Mumbles in 1975). There a father, son and grandson, all called Abraham Ace, were the keepers for three-quarters of a century.

The first Abraham Ace, lightkeeper, was born in 1779 in Penrice on the Gower Peninsula to Abraham, a ship's carpenter and his wife, Elizabeth (née Loyd). He followed in his father's footsteps to become a shipwright, but relocated to Devon, where he married Sarah Speree in Plymouth. All their children were born there, including the youngest, Abraham, born in 1820. In the late 1830s the first Abraham and some of the family moved back to South Wales, where he took over keeping the Mumbles lighthouse from Benjamin Llewellyn, who had run it for more than thirty years. In the meantime, the second Abraham had become a mariner and married Margaret McLean from Glasgow. They were also living at the lighthouse and over the years took on more lighthouse responsibilities. In 1849 his father retired after having been injured in a fall, and the Swansea Harbour Trust appointed Abraham Jr as the keeper, after considering six candidates.

Abraham Jr and Margaret had seven children, including another Abraham, who was born in 1842 and received his mate's certificate in the merchant marine service in 1865. The next year he married Sarah Hixon in Swansea and they too took up residence at the lighthouse. After his father's death in 1885 Abraham III became the main lighthouse keeper at Mumbles. On his death in 1903 the lighthouse passed out of the family's custodianship, to Assistant Keeper Jasper Williams and later John Thomas.

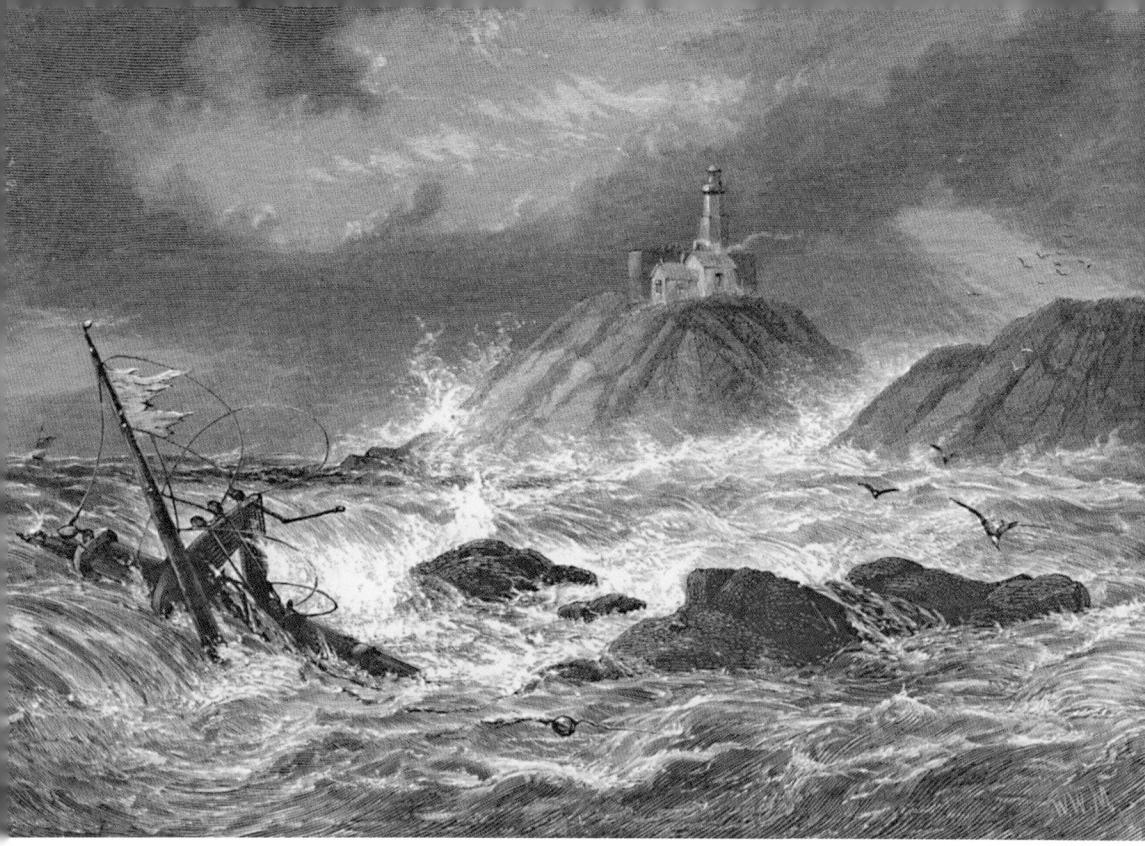

Shipwreck near the Mumbles lighthouse, *c.* 1875. (W. W. May)

The Ace family are best known, however, for the heroism of two of the daughters. Among the seven children of the second Abraham were Jessie and her older sister Margaret. On 27 January 1883 the German barque *Admiral Prinz Adalbert* was driven onto the rocks near the lighthouse in a fierce storm. The lifeboat *Wolverhampton* was launched to rescue the mariners, but it was swamped by a wave and the lifeboat crew thrown into the water. Four lost their lives, but the sisters were able to clamber down to the rocks and throw a rope to rescue two of them.

The story of their part in the rescue spread; they featured on the cover of *The Graphic* illustrated newspaper, Queen Victoria requested a photograph of Jessie as a memento and Clement Scott composed a poem, 'The Women of Mumbles Head'. The sisters were given awards from the Board of Trade, along with other rescuers, and the Empress of Germany sent them gold and gem brooches in recognition of their bravery. A Blue Plaque was erected in 2016 on Mumbles Pier, overlooking the lighthouse, to commemorate them.

Another tale of rescues at lighthouses centres on Ynys Llanddwyn, a tidal island off the south coast of Anglesey. A daymark tower called Twr Bach, which acted as a landmark guiding mariners into the Menai Strait towards Caernarfon port, has graced the southern tip of the island since the early nineteenth century, along with a set of cottages to house pilots who would guide the ships past the dangerous sand bars into the strait. A new tower, Twr Mawr, was built on higher ground nearby and in 1846 was turned into a proper

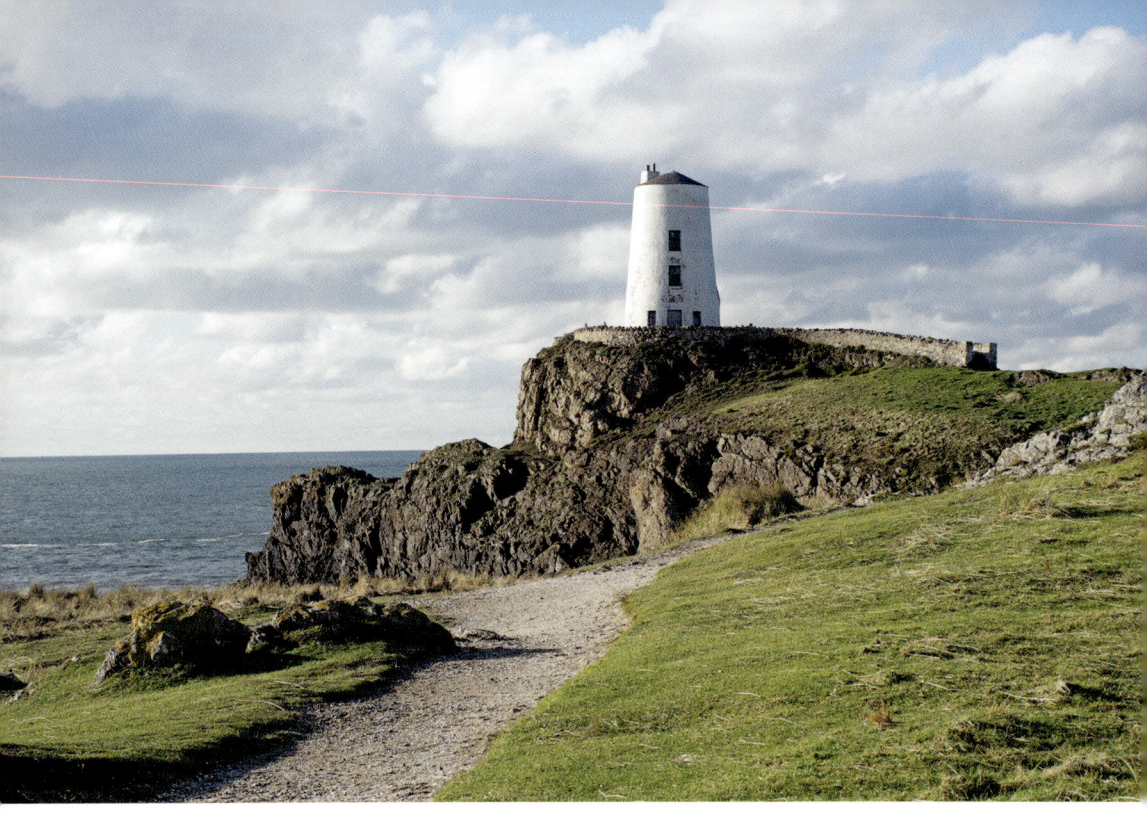

Tŵr Mawr lighthouse, Llanddwyn Island, Anglesey.

lighthouse with a lamp shining out the seaward window. The four pilots stationed there would also take turns tending the lamp in the lighthouse.

The most famous of the pilots and keepers of Llanddwyn was Elizabeth Jones, who was born and grew up on the island. Her father was Thomas Williams, who was appointed as a pilot following the tragic death of three of the pilots in January 1874, when their boat capsized after having guided a ship out of harbour. In 1898 she married William Jones, who had become a pilot there four years earlier, and they had five children.

After being immersed in piloting and light-keeping all her life, Elizabeth was well placed to take over when her husband died in 1918. She reportedly was a strong woman, both physically and in terms of willpower, and was officially appointed as a pilot.

In 1940, at the age of sixty-five, Elizabeth was involved in two rescues of the crew of ships sinking off the Llanddwyn coast. During the second she plunged into the water to bring a young man ashore. The next year she and other rescuers were invited to Buckingham Palace to receive awards from the queen. The press dubbed her the 'Grace Darling of Anglesey', after the famous lighthouse keeper's daughter from Northumberland who was immortalised for her part in a sea rescue.

Not only was she a good pilot but Elizabeth was also a keen lover of the wildlife of the island. In 1911 the Royal Society for the Protection of Birds set up a nature reserve on the island to protect the roseate terns that nested there. She and her husband acted as the wardens, monitoring the birds and watching out for egg thieves. She continued with her custodianship of the island for the rest of her life. When at Buckingham Palace the queen asked her if she got lonely on the island. She said, 'No, I've got the birds for company.' She promoted the wonders of nature on Llanddwyn through welcoming visitors to the island as well as broadcasting about the bird life from the BBC Radio studios in Bangor.

This section started off with a mention of the 2016 film *The Lighthouse*, based on a true story of events at the Smalls lighthouse, off the Pembrokeshire coast. In 1801 the original timber-piled Smalls lighthouse was manned by two keepers, Thomas Howell and Thomas

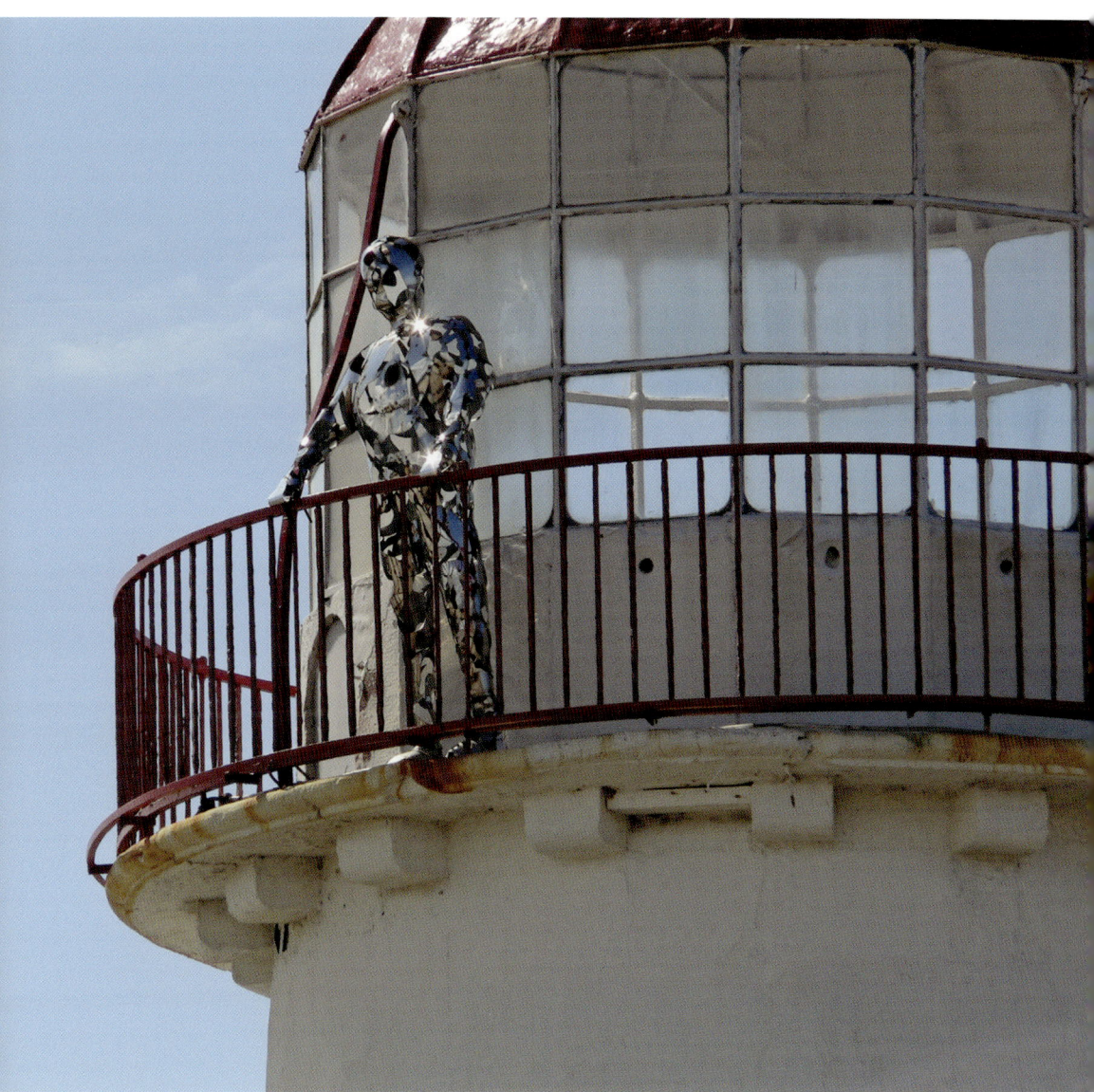

The Keeper, a sculpture by Angela Smith installed at Point of Ayr in 2010, based on stories of a ghost at the lighthouse. (Wikimedia CC BY-SA 2.0/Mat Fascione)

Griffith. Although they were known to dislike each other, they were cooped up in a tower on a rock a long distance from the coast. Griffith fell ill and eventually died a long time before their scheduled relief by new keepers. Howell raised distress signals that were seen by passing ships, but stormy weather prevented any attempts to land at the rock.

After living beside the decaying body of his departed companion for several days Howell needed to take action. He couldn't just bury the body at sea, as their known animosities could lead to him being accused of murder. Howells constructed a coffin for Griffith's body and placed it outside on the gallery of the lantern. It remained there for many weeks until a rescue boat was eventually able to land. By that time Howell had been driven insane. After this incident it was required that isolated lighthouses always had three keepers.

Almost a century later the scene was almost played out again, as distress signals were spotted at the Smalls during stormy weather in January 1894. A tender was sent out to determine what the problem was but couldn't land in the gales. However, signals from the lighthouse indicated that Principal Keeper Justion Sibert was ill. Repeated attempts to reach the lighthouse were regularly reported in the local newspapers until finally, almost three weeks later, he was rescued to be treated for bowel inflammation by the Trinity House medical officer.

CHAPTER 5

The Future

Through this book we've travelled the long history of lighthouses and their developments in Wales. Advances in technology meant that fewer tasks were required of the keepers, up to the point where all lighthouses in Wales today are automated and unmanned. Instead, a local attendant and a team of technicians monitor and maintain the lights. Even though the full-time keepers living at the tower are long gone, the lights still shine brightly.

When showing visitors around South Stack I've regularly been asked 'why do we still need lighthouses, when the ships have satellite GPS and other technology?' As anyone who uses modern gadgets will know, electronics are fallible. The software or hardware can develop faults, or the entire electrical system can fail.

Lighthouses and other beacons serve as reliable physical landmarks. An experienced mariner with a map will know exactly where they are with these and other land-based features. If someone is navigating with GPS and encounters an unexpected lighthouse, or fails to see one that should be present, it indicates that something has gone wrong. A recent review by the General Lighthouse Authorities (the group of three authorities responsible for lighthouses in Britain and Ireland: the Commissioners of Irish Lights, the Northern Lighthouse Board and Trinity House) states:

> There is an identifiable increase in marine accidents resulting from misuse of and over reliance on electronic display systems and technology for navigation and passage planning. In a number of instances a series of clearly identifiable aids to navigation have been ignored in the run up to a serious incident.

The same review gives their mission statement as: 'To deliver a reliable, efficient and cost effective Aids to Navigation Service for the benefit and safety of all mariners.' They are committed to maintaining lighthouses as a key part of the maritime infrastructure and are following a programme of modernising them for the twenty-first century. Solar power is widely used, and existing lamps are being replaced with low-power and long-life LEDs. When these are installed in lighthouses that relied on rotating Fresnel lenses to produce the flash, the optics that float on highly toxic mercury baths are being removed. Mindful of their heritage value, the authorities look for new homes for these beautiful instruments.

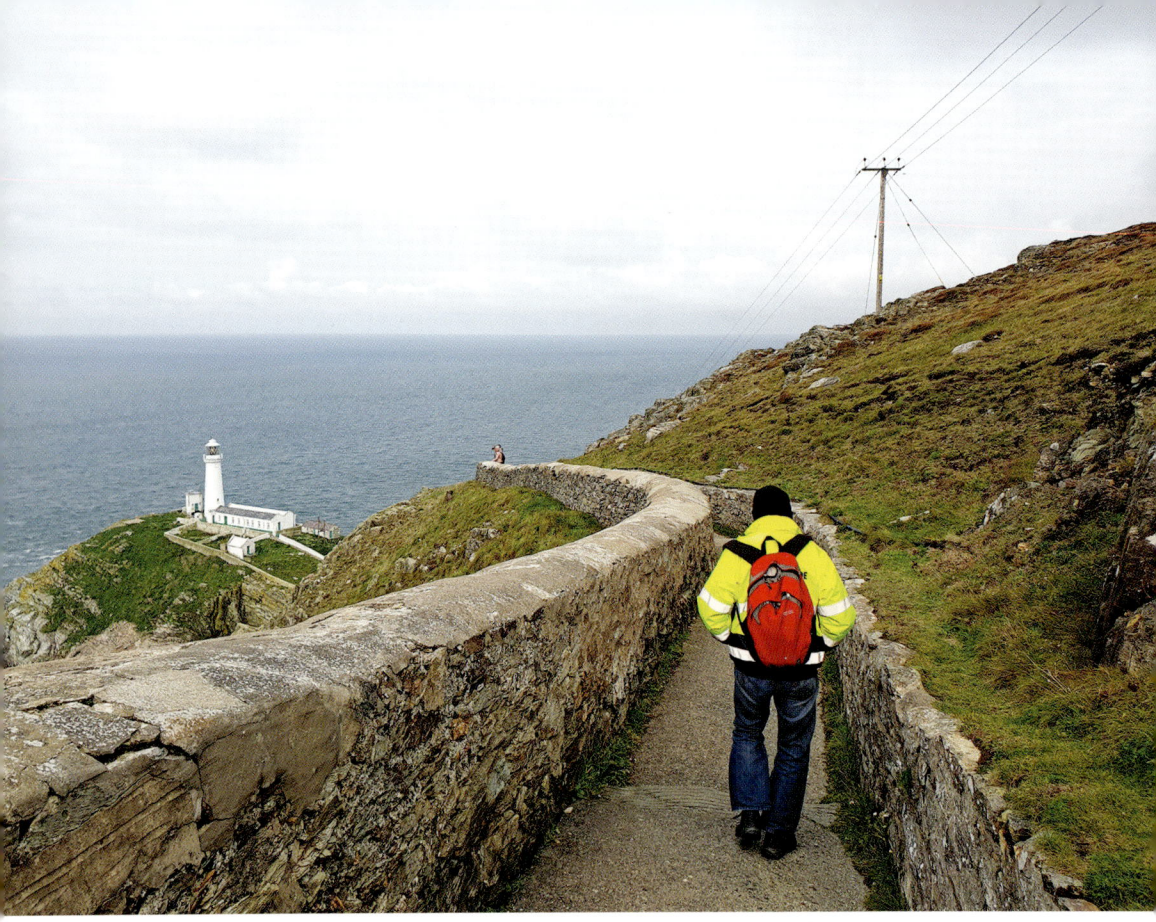

The author walks down the 400 steps to South Stack lighthouse to start his shift as a tour guide. (Catherine Duigan)

The legacy of these evocative structures is also a key part of their future. People have been visiting lighthouses for centuries to marvel at their beauty and ingenuity. They feature on countless postcards, numerous paintings and photographs, and many travelogues. They act as a counterpoint to the landscapes and seascapes that surround them and intrigue visitors with their history. The keepers would regularly show visitors around, proudly showing off their domain. Today South Stack is the only lighthouse in Wales generally open for the public to climb the tower, with many thousands visiting each year, but most others can be admired from nearby.

As the keepers left, their accommodations became available to be purchased by people looking for unusual homes or for rental to holidaymakers. In Wales you can stay at the keeper's cottages at Nash Point, St Ann's Head, Point Lynas and Penmon/Trwyn Du. At Great Orme the lighthouse that was made redundant in 1985 has been turned into a B&B, where you can sleep in the lantern room as well as other rooms in the building. West Usk is now a private home but has often been a B&B since its closure in 1922 and currently one of the outbuildings can be rented by visitors. Skokholm lighthouse houses the warden of the island's nature reserve.

The heritage of lighthouses can also be explored via museums and other public displays. A visit to South Stack includes a walk through the machine room, where various pieces of old equipment are on display alongside interpretation panels. The Holyhead Maritime Museum has many lighthouse-related objects, including a working scale model of the Holyhead Breakwater lighthouse. The original Fresnel lens from Great Orme can be viewed in the exhibition on the summit of the Orme and the Bardsey optic is on display at the Porth y Swnt visitor centre in Aberdaron, Llŷn. In South Wales the Helwick lightship can be seen in the marina after visiting the maritime displays inside the nearby National Waterfront Museum. Further afield, the Association of Lighthouse Keepers maintains a museum at Hurst Castle near Milford on Sea in Hampshire, England, and the Museum of Scottish Lighthouses is located at Fraserburgh, Scotland.

Lighthouses capture the imagination and can act as a metaphor for many ambitions and attributes. They represent guidance, safety and hope, especially in the face of adversity. They also symbolise strength, resilience and the ability to withstand storms. Numerous organisations offering leadership guidance, mental health support and charitable assistance have adopted the lighthouse in their names and logos.

They have also inspired all sorts of creative endeavours. There have been dozens of movies with 'lighthouse' in the title. Writers such as Virginia Woolf, P. D. James and Jeanette Winterson have used lighthouses as centrepieces to their plots. The former National Poet of Wales Gillian Clarke's poem 'The Lighthouse' celebrates the structure where 'the great fish-eye revolves / in a socket that floats on mercury'. The tower on isolated Bardsey Island features regularly in the poems of Christine Evans, who has lived there for decades.

Factual books about lighthouses abound. A wide range of these can be found in the Further Reading section. Most prominent is *Lighthouses – Their Architecture, History and Archaeology*, by the late Aberystwyth-based industrial archaeologist Douglas B. Hague and his partner Rosemary Christie. After becoming enamoured with the lighthouse on Bardsey while there in 1960 surveying for the Royal Commission on the Ancient and Historical Monuments of Wales, Hague began learning all he could about the structures. Soon joined by Christie, for a decade they both travelled Britain, Ireland and Continental Europe, visiting lighthouses and consulting archives to produce a comprehensive account of their history and architectural features.

Lighthouses inspire music too. Peter Maxwell Davies composed a chamber opera called *The Lighthouse*, based on the true story of three keepers disappearing from the lighthouse on the Flannan Islands, Orkney. His successor as Master of the Queen's/King's Music, Errolyn Wallen, actually lives in a lighthouse at Strathy Point, near Thurso, where she composed *The Lighthouse Wave* and *The Lighthouse Keeper* amongst other pieces. On 22 June 2013 fifty ships and three brass bands with sixty-five musicians gathered at Souter lighthouse in South Tyneside to perform *Foghorn Requiem*, composed by Orlando Gough, where the brass instruments were joined by the horns on the ships and the deep bellowing of the Souter foghorn itself (foghornrequiem.org). The lighthouse lends its name to popular music groups such as the Canadian rock band Lighthouse, the British pop-soul duo The Lighthouse Family and the 1970s group Edison Lighthouse (taking their name from Eddystone). Top international artists James Taylor, Westlife, Stevie Nicks, Pulp and many more have released lighthouse-themed songs, and in Wales the lighthouse features in pieces like *Music For Smalls Lighthouse* by Michael Tanner/Plinth and 'Ceidwad y Goleudy' by Bryn Fon.

While writing this book I have travelled up and down Wales to see all the lighthouses, as well as further afield, tracking down lights on the Isle of Man, England, Ireland and the Hudson Valley, New England and the Great Lakes in the USA. They are fascinating structures often in inspirational settings, and I never tire of exploring a new one. I hope that this book will inspire you to explore more about these evocative and historic structures.

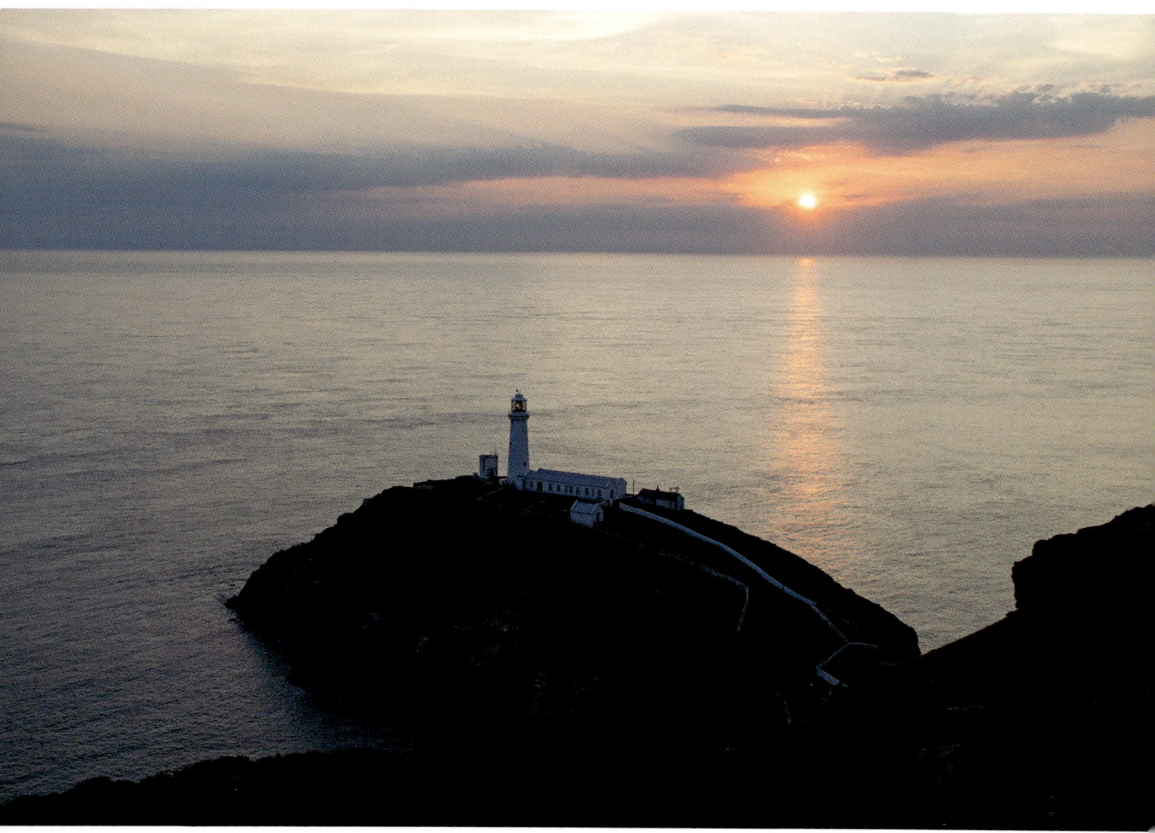

Sunset at South Stack.

Appendix

The Lighthouses

The tables overleaf give the basic information about the lighthouses in Wales. Each entry gives the location (as Ordnance Survey Grid References, latitude/longitude and What3Words (what3words.com)), the year the light was first established and any subsequent rebuilding, and of automation and closure. The height of the tower and the height above sea level of the light source is also given in metres, as is the range of the

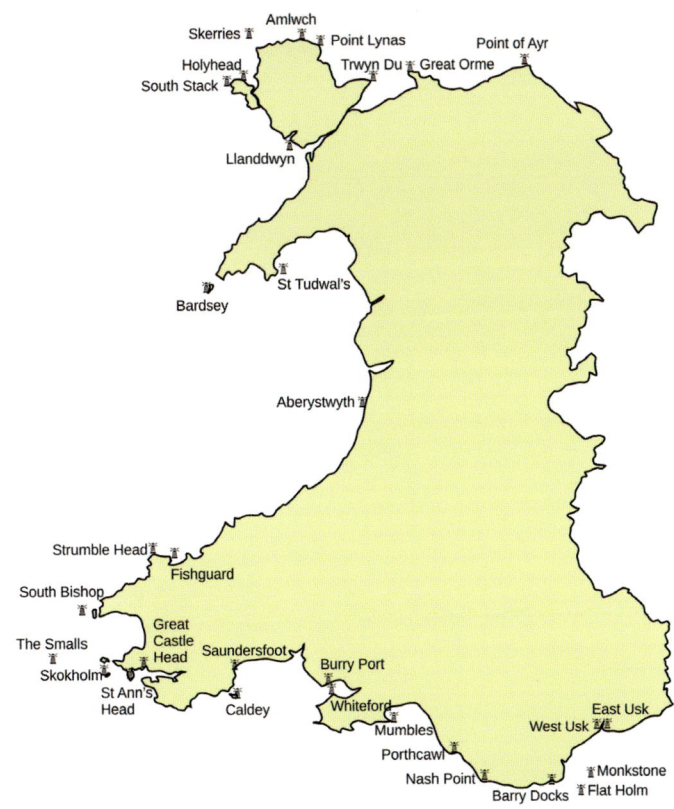

Map of the lighthouses of Wales.

light in kilometres. For active lights its character and type of optic (at the time of writing in 2025) are also given.

The locations of the lighthouses are shown on the map on the previous page. You can also see the exact location on a Google map located at tinyurl.com/LighthousesOfWales or on my website lighthouses.wales. The website also has further details about and photographs of all the lighthouses.

Lighthouse Character Abbreviations

Each lighthouse will have a specific character, or pattern of the light, that is distinct from others in the area, so they can be told apart. It can be described with a few abbreviations, which are used on sea charts to identify the different lights. The abbreviation consists of three main elements: the type of light (e.g. flashing or fixed), the colour of the light and the period of time for the cycling of the light pattern. The abbreviations used in the following tables are:

Type of light: F – Fixed (always on), Fl – Flashing (light on periodically, but off for a much longer period), Oc – Occulting (like flashing, but period of light is longer than darkness), Q – Quick light (flashing rapidly, more than thirty times a minute). If the flashing or occulting occurs more than once in a sequence the number of times is included in parentheses (e.g. Fl (2) means it flashes twice).

Colour of light: W – white, R – red, G – green, Bu - blue. For white-only lights this is left out. If more than one colour is included this means that different colours are displayed in different directions (e.g. a white light is visible when in safe waters, but green or red when in areas that might not be safely navigable).

Period: The timing of the cycle of the light pattern (e.g. Fl 10s means a flash occurs every ten seconds).

Lighthouses of Wales

Point of Ayr/Talacre (Goleudy'r Parlwr Du)	
Location	SJ 12099 85267 / 53.3570, -3.3222 / dignify. conducted.overdrive
Established / Rebuilt / Automated / Closed	1777 / c. 1820 / –– / 1844
Height of tower (m) / above sea level (m)	18 / 16

Great Orme (Pen y Gogarth)	
Location	SH 75673 84447 / 53.3423, -3.8689 / elbow. craftsmen.activism
Established / Rebuilt / Automated / Closed	1862 / –– / –– / 1985
Height of tower (m) / above sea level (m)	11 / 99

Trwyn Du/Penmon	
Location	SH 64148 81499 / 53.3130, -4.0406 / verb.cringes.slows
Established / Rebuilt / Automated / Closed	1838 / –– / 1922 / ––
Height of tower (m) / above sea level (m) / Range (km)	22 / 19 / 22
Character	Fl 5s
Optic	LED, 2021 (previously first order fixed catadioptric)

Point Lynas (Goleudy Trwyn y Balog or Goleudy Pwynt Leinws)	
Location	SH 47957 93501 / 53.4163, -4.2892 / thrusters.flinch.divide
Established / Rebuilt / Automated / Closed	1779 / 1835 / 1989 / ––
Height of tower (m) / above sea level (m) / Range (km)	11 / 39 / 33
Character	Oc 10s
Optic	Second order fixed catadioptric

Amlwch Port (Porth Amlwch)	
Location	SH 45044 93491 / 53.4154, -4.3330 / stretcher.thrashed.tests
Established / Rebuilt / Automated / Closed	1793 / 1853 / –– / c. 1972
Height of tower (m) / above sea level (m)	11 / ––

Skerries (Ynysoedd y Moelrhoniaid)	
Location	SH 26776 94772 / 53.4212, -4.6083 / occur.supported.segmented
Established / Rebuilt / Automated / Closed	1717 / 1759, 1804, 1848 / 1987 / ––
Height of tower (m) / above sea level (m) / Range (km)	23 / 36 / 33
Character	Fl(2) 15s
Optic	LED, 2025 (previously first order rotating catadioptric)

Holyhead Admiralty Pier, Salt Island (Caergybi, Ynys Halen)	
Location	SH 25564 82904 / 53.3143, -4.6199 / status. tennis.dolly
Established / Rebuilt / Automated / Closed	1821 / –– / –– / 1870s
Height of tower (m) / above sea level (m)	15 / ––

Holyhead Breakwater (Morglawdd Caergybi)	
Location	SH 25676 84756 / 53.3309, -4.6193 / gracing.silks.booth
Established / Rebuilt / Automated / Closed	1873 / –– / 1961 / ––
Height of tower (m) / above sea level (m) / Range (km)	19 / 21 / 26
Character	Fl(3) G 10s
Optic	LED

South Stack (Ynys Lawd)	
Location	SH 20242 82262 / 53.3067, -4.6993 / divide. live.florists
Established / Rebuilt / Automated / Closed	1809 / –– / 1984 / ––
Height of tower (m) / above sea level (m) / Range (km)	28 / 60 / 44
Character	Fl 10s
Optic	First order rotating catadioptric

Tŵr Bach, Llanddwyn	
Location	SH 38674 62400 / 53.1343, -4.4130 / wires. lurching.decrease
Established / Rebuilt / Automated / Closed	c. 1800–18 / –– / 1975 / ––
Height of tower (m) / above sea level (m) / Range (km)	5 / 12 / 13
Character	Fl WR 2.5s
Optic	LED

Tŵr Mawr, Llanddwyn	
Location	SH 38515 62512 / 53.1352, -4.4154 / recline. doted.flop
Established / Rebuilt / Automated / Closed	1846 / –– / –– / 1975
Height of tower (m) / above sea level (m)	11 / ––

Bardsey (Ynys Enlli)

Location	SH 11145 20604 / 52.7500, -4.7996 / fuel. invest.headstone
Established / Rebuilt / Automated / Closed	1821 / — / 1987 / —
Height of tower (m) / above sea level (m) / Range (km)	30 / 39 / 33
Character	Fl R 10s
Optic	LED, 2014 (previously first order rotating catadioptric)

St Tudwal's (Ynys Tudwal Fawr)

Location	SH 33495 25191 / 52.7985, -4.4712 / flops. perch.album
Established / Rebuilt / Automated / Closed	1877 / — / 1922 / —
Height of tower (m) / above sea level (m) / Range (km)	11 / 46 / 26
Character	Fl WR 15s
Optic	LED, 2022, inside second order fixed catadioptric

Aberystwyth, Ceredigion

Location	SN 57790 80815 / 52.4068, -4.0920 / impact.prettiest.scream
Established / Rebuilt / Automated / Closed	1990s / — / — / —
Height of tower (m) / above sea level (m)	7 / 12
Character	Fl(2) WG 10s
Optic	LED

Fishguard Breakwater North (Abergwaun)

Location	SM 96254 39095 / 52.0128, -4.9704 / twitchy.perfume.forklift
Established / Rebuilt / Automated / Closed	1906 / late 1910s / ? / —
Height of tower (m) / above sea level (m) / Range (km)	14 / 18 / 24
Character	Fl G 4.5s
Optic	

Strumble Head (Ynys Meicel)

Location	SM 89236 41285 / 52.0298, -5.0738 / sands. confining.trombone
Established / Rebuilt / Automated / Closed	1908 / –– / 1980 / ––
Height of tower (m) / above sea level (m) / Range (km)	17 / 45 / 48
Character	Fl(4) 15s
Optic	First order rotating catadioptric

South Bishop (Emsger)

Location	SM 65103 22632 / 51.8527, -5.4122 / castaways.relishes.volatiles
Established / Rebuilt / Automated / Closed	1839 / –– / 1983 / ––
Height of tower (m) / above sea level (m) / Range (km)	11 / 44 / 30
Character	Fl 5s
Optic	Fourth order rotating catadioptric

Smalls

Location	SM 46617 08861 / 51.7211, -5.6700 / angled. soundboard.boulevards
Established / Rebuilt / Automated / Closed	1776 / 1861 / 1987 / ––
Height of tower (m) / above sea level (m) / Range (km)	42 / 36 / 33
Character	Fl(3) 15s
Optic	First order rotating catadioptric

Skokholm (Ynys Sgogwm)

Location	SM 72932 04573 / 51.6939, -5.2869 / nicer. bonds.extensives
Established / Rebuilt / Automated / Closed	1916 / –– / 1983 / ––
Height of tower (m) / above sea level (m) / Range (km)	18 / 54 / 15
Character	Fl WR 10s
Optic	LED, 2012 (previously fourth order rotating catadioptric)

St Ann's Head Low (Penrhyn Santes Ann)

Location	SM 80691 02831 / 51.6813, -5.1738 / statement.cheaper.tablets
Established / Rebuilt / Automated / Closed	1662 / 1800, 1844 / 1998 / ---
Height of tower (m) / above sea level (m) / Range (km)	13 / 48 / 33
Character	Fl WR 5s
Optic	First order fixed catadioptric

St Ann's Head High (Penrhyn Santes Ann)

Location	SM 80574 02958 / 51.6824, -5.1755 / truckload.grumbles.grit
Established / Rebuilt / Automated / Closed	1662 / 1714, 1800 / --- / 1910
Height of tower (m)	23

Great Castle Head (Pen y Castell Mawr)

Location	SM 84713 05985 / 51.7112, -5.1176 / cracking.frostbite.robot
Established / Rebuilt / Automated / Closed	1870 / --- / ? / ---
Height of tower (m) / above sea level (m) / Range (km)	5 / 27 / 9
Character	F WRG
Optic	Sealed beam lights on roof

Caldey (Ynys Bŷr)

Location	SS 14319 95945 / 51.6316, -4.6843 / ticked.typically.wanted
Established / Rebuilt / Automated / Closed	1829 / --- / 1927 / ---
Height of tower (m) / above sea level (m) / Range (km)	16 / 65 / 24
Character	Fl(3) WR 20s
Optic	Second order fixed catadioptric

Saundersfoot (Llanusyllt)

Location	SN 13865 04662 / 51.7097, -4.6955 / dreamers.lanes.disbelief
Established / Rebuilt / Automated / Closed	1848 / 1954 / ? / ––
Height of tower (m) / above sea level (m) / Range (km)	5 / 6 / 13
Character	Fl R 5s
Optic	LED

Burry Port (Porth Tywyn)

Location	SN 44444 00036 / 51.6775, -4.2512 / agreeing.slogged.eternally
Established / Rebuilt / Automated / Closed	1842 / –– / ? / ––
Height of tower (m) / above sea level (m) / Range (km)	6 / 7 / 13
Character	Fl 5s
Optic	LED

Whiteford Point (Llanmadog)

Location	SS 44366 97266 / 51.6526, -4.2511 / squeaks.willpower.tuck
Established / Rebuilt / Automated / Closed	1854 / 1866 / 1919 / 1921
Height of tower (m) / above sea level (m)	13.5 / ––

Mumbles (Mwmbwls)

Location	SS 63476 87170 / 51.5668, -3.9712 / dabble.forest.roosters
Established / Rebuilt / Automated / Closed	1794 / –– / 1934 / ––
Height of tower (m) / above sea level (m) / Range (km)	17 / 35 / 28
Character	Fl(4) 20s
Optic	LED, 2017 (previously first order fixed catadioptric)

Porthcawl

Location	SS 82044 76274 / 51.4731, -3.6997 / collision.footballers.dragons
Established / Rebuilt / Automated / Closed	1866 / 1911 / ? / —
Height of tower (m) / above sea level (m) / Range (km)	9 / 10 / 11
Character	F WGR
Optic	LED

Nash Point Low (Trwyn yr As)

Location	SS 91840 68060 / 51.4012, -3.5562 / fussy.bucks.exulted
Established / Rebuilt / Automated / Closed	1832 / — / — / 1920s
Height of tower (m) / above sea level (m)	25 / —

Nash Point High (Trwyn yr As)

Location	SS 92132 68026 / 51.4010, -3.5520 / golf.failed.third
Established / Rebuilt / Automated / Closed	1832 / — / 1998 / —
Height of tower (m) / above sea level (m) / Range (km)	37 / 56 / 39
Character	Fl(2) WR 15s
Optic	360mm rotating catadioptric

Barry Docks (Dociau'r Barri)

Location	ST 12526 66543 / 51.3912, -3.2586 / noting.waddled.boost
Established / Rebuilt / Automated / Closed	1890 / — / ? / —
Height of tower (m) / above sea level (m) / Range (km)	9 / 12 / 18
Character	Fl 2.5s
Optic	

Flat Holm (Ynys Echni)	
Location	ST 22241 64663 / 51.3757, -3.1186 / decking.youths.eagle
Established / Rebuilt / Automated / Closed	1737 / 1820, 1866 / 1988 / —
Height of tower (m) / above sea level (m) / Range (km)	30 / 50 / 28
Character	Fl(3) WR 10s
Optic	LED, within first order fixed catadioptric

Monkstone	
Location	ST 23599 69026 / 51.4151, -3.1000 / breached.meatballs.stilted
Established / Rebuilt / Automated / Closed	1839 / 1859, 1903, 1925, 1993 / — / —
Height of tower (m) / above sea level (m) / Range (km)	23 / 13 / 22
Character	Fl 5s
Optic	LED

West Usk/St Brides Wentlooge (Gorllewin Wysg, Gwynllŵg)	
Location	ST 31113 82883 / 51.5406, -2.9947 / conned.reflector.tickets
Established / Rebuilt / Automated / Closed	1820 / — / — / 1922
Height of tower (m) / above sea level (m)	17 / —

East Usk (Dwyrain Wysg, Trefonnen)	
Location	ST 33033 82787 / 51.5400, -2.9670 / escaping.polishing.moves
Established / Rebuilt / Automated / Closed	1893 / — / 1893 / —
Height of tower (m) / above sea level (m) / Range (km)	11 / 11 / 20
Character	Fl(2) WRG 10s
Optic	Electric beacon

Further Reading and Information

Books

Allan, Jennifer Lucy, *The Foghorn's Lament – The Disappearing Music of the Coast* (London: White Rabbit, 2021), 295 pp. – music journalist Allan discovers the power of the foghorn and goes on an odyssey to discover all she can about them.

Dora, Veronica Della, *Where Light in Darkness Lies: The Story of the Lighthouse* (London: Reaktion Books, 2022), 277 pp. – a fascinating account of how lighthouses feature in literature, art and the human imagination.

Farrah, Robert W. E., *From the Lighthouse – A Lighthouse Keeper's Memoir* (Dumfries & Galloway: Hayloft Publishing, 2025), 240 pp. – the journal kept by keeper Farrah during his time at Nash Point, Trevose Head and Alderney/Mannez lighthouses, 1995–97.

Hague, Douglas B. and Christie, Rosemary, *Lighthouses – Their Architecture, History and Archaeology* (Llandysul: Gomer Press, 1975), 333 pp. – a comprehensive survey of the history and architecture of lighthouses around the world.

Hague, Douglas B., *Lighthouses of Wales – Their Architecture and Archaeology* (Aberystwyth: Royal Commission on the Ancient & Historical Monuments of Wales, 1994), 104pp. – another book by the industrial archaeologist Hague, focusing on the lighthouses of Wales. Out of print but still available as a download at shop.rcahmw.gov.uk.

Jackson, Derrick, *Lighthouses of England and Wales* (Newton Abbot: David & Charles, 1975), 176 pp. – a tour around the lighthouses of England and Wales, illustrated with numerous pen and ink drawings by the author.

Jones, Ian, *Ynys Lawd - Goleudy Enwog Môn/South Stack – Anglesey's Famous Lighthouse* (Llangefni: Isle of Anglesey County Council, 2009), 84 pp. – an excellent and comprehensive history of this iconic lighthouse.

Lane, Anthony and Augustus, Martin, *Lightships – Their Design, Development and Diversity* (Stroud: Amberley Publishing, 2024), 96 pp. – documents the history of lightships around the British coast with numerous historic photos and detailed diagrams.

Leach, Nicholas and Denton, Tony, *Lighthouses of Wales* (Lichfield: Foxglove Publishing Ltd, 2011), 96 pp. – descriptions of thirty-eight lighthouses of Wales, well-illustrated with colour photos.

Leach, Nicholas and Denton, Tony, *Lighthouses of England and Wales* (Cheltenham: The History Press, 2018), 336 pp. – a larger format book covering all of England and Wales.

Nancollas, Tom, *Seashaken Houses: A Lighthouse History from Eddystone to Fastnet* (London: Penguin, 2018), 227 pp. – the author travels to several of the remote offshore tower lighthouses around Britain and Ireland to tell the stories of their building and manning.

O'Reilly, Roger, *Legendary Lighthouses of Britain* (London: Watkins, 2024), 224 pp. – a tour of the lighthouses of Britain, supplemented by the author's retro travel poster-style illustrations and other sketches.

Parker, Tony, *Lighthouse* (London: Eland, 2006), 296 pp. – an oral historian talks to lighthouse keepers, and their families, about their lives.

Peppitt, Ed, *The Beacon Bike* (London: Icon Books, 2024), 319 pp. – after being diagnosed with multiple sclerosis, lighthouse enthusiast Peppitt sets out to cycle to all 327 lighthouses on the coast of Wales and England.

Robinson, John and Diane, *Lighthouses of Liverpool Bay* (Stroud: Tempus Publishing, 2007), 191 pp. – a detailed history of the numerous lighthouses that guided ships into Liverpool port.

Woodman, Richard and Wilson, Jane, *The Lighthouses of Trinity House* (Bradford on Avon: Thomas Reed Publications, 2002), 256 pp. – a coffee table-sized book, produced in conjunction with Trinity House, covering all their lighthouses.

Websites

'A Lighthouse Keeper's guided tours' (youtube.com/@PeterHalil) – a large collection of videos by former lighthouse keeper Peter Halil, visiting lights around the country and telling their stories.

Association of Lighthouse Keepers (alk.org.uk) – an organization originally founded for current and former lighthouse workers, but now a forum for anyone interested in lighthouses.

Pharology website (pharology.eu) – an excellent and comprehensive website about all things related to lighthouses, developed by Ken Trethewey.

Trinity House website (trinityhouse.co.uk/lighthouses-and-lightvessels) – up-to-date details of the lighthouses and lightvessels maintained by them.

Acknowledgements

I'd like to thank the following for their help in researching and writing this book:

Chris Christie for permission to use illustrations and other materials from the work on lighthouses by Douglas Hague and Rosemary Christie.

Frank and Danielle Sheahan, owners of West Usk lighthouse, Stephen and Mandy Pickles, owners of Bidston lighthouse in the Wirral, Fiona and Ray Kilpatrick, owners of the Great Orme lighthouse, and Richard Brown, warden on Skokholm island, for their hospitality in allowing me to visit the lighthouses.

The Association of Lighthouse Keepers (ALK) and the all the members I've met at events who stoked my interest in lighthouses.

Mandy and Stephen Pickles for their help as I explored the ALK archives at Bidston lighthouse.

All my fellow tour guides at South Stack lighthouse for the camaraderie and interesting discussions.

The National Library of Wales for access to papers of Douglas Hague and Rosemary Christie, as well as other lighthouse-related documents.

I'd particularly like to thank my wife, Catherine Duigan, for her help and encouragement in writing this book, chauffeuring as I navigated to various lighthouses around the coast, accompanying me on long walks to remote lighthouses, reading and commenting on the manuscript, and lots of discussions and observations as we worked side-by-side as guides at South Stack lighthouse.

All modern photos were taken by me, except where otherwise noted. Uncredited older images are from my collections. Images credited to RCAHMW are Crown copyright and are reproduced with the permission of the Royal Commission on the Ancient and Historical Monuments of Wales (RCAHMW), under delegated authority from The Keeper of Public Records. Every attempt has been made to seek permission for copyright material used in this book. However, if we have inadvertently used copyright material without permission/acknowledgement, we apologise and we will make the necessary correction at the earliest opportunity.

About the Author

Warren Kovach is the author of the popular Anglesey-History.co.uk website, which highlights aspects of the island's history, supplemented by many of his own photographs. He has also written three previous books for Amberley: *Anglesey Through Time*, *Anglesey in 50 Buildings* and *A–Z of the Isle of Anglesey*. He has been a regular tour guide at South Stack lighthouse on Anglesey.

Born and raised in Ohio, USA, he moved to Anglesey in the early 1990s and soon set about exploring its history and landscape. He has a PhD as a researcher in biology, ecology and palaeontology, but later moved to developing scientific computer software. He is a keen photographer and has had his photos published in many national newspapers, books and magazines around the world.

You can follow him on various social media platforms as @angleseyhistory (or @AngleseyHist on X) or @lighthousewales for lighthouse-related posts.